TO DAD
75th BIRTHDAY FROM
STUART KAREN
CHARLEY DEC 3th - 08
BEST WISHES

Staghunting on Exmoor

1940-1998

Staghunting
on
Exmoor
1940-1998

ROBIN DUNN

RARE BOOKS AND BERRY
2008

This edition first published in 2008 by

Rare Books and Berry
High Street, Porlock,
Minehead, Somerset
TA24 8PT

www.rarebooksandberry.co.uk

A CIP catalogue record for this title is
available from the British Library

ISBN 978-0-9539951-9-6

Designed and typeset in Minion by
Alacrity, Sandford, Somerset

Printed and bound by
Biddles Ltd, King's Lynn

Acknowledgements

LAST YEAR my wife said to me, "Now that we are approaching our ninetieth birthdays and you are unable to hunt or garden you must find something to occupy you, otherwise you will be intolerable to live with. So why don't you write another book?" I had long thought that another book ought to be written to bring the history of the Devon & Somerset Staghounds up to date. I consulted Dick Lloyd, who said, "Why don't you write it yourself?" So here it is. I am indebted to him for the use of his capacious file of records of the Hunt going back to 1946 and also to him and his brother Pat for the loan of photographs. Rosemary Pile, Chairman of the Hunt Club, has also allowed me to use photographs, especially of the period when her husband Donald was the harbourer. But my main source of photographs has been Michael Hesman of Ilfracombe (telephone 01271-862421), a regular car follower who has a wonderful collection going back to the 1970s, some of which have been reproduced here. I take full responsibility for the text, including any errors, and am grateful to Diana Scott, MSH, my daughter Janie Clifford, and my wife Joan for their suggestions and support.

Contents

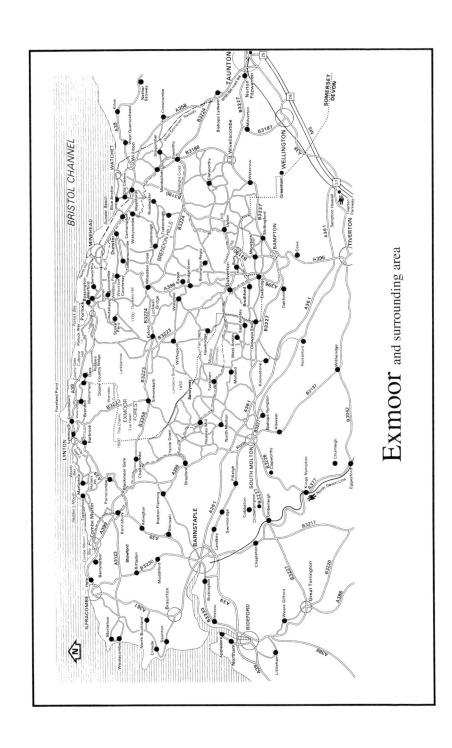

Exmoor and surrounding area

CHAPTER I

Wartime Hunting

MY FIRST day's staghunting was on Thursday 19 September 1940. The meet was at Hawkcombe Head and it was an auspicious day for me in more ways than one. I had returned in early June from Dunkirk, and the Battle of Britain was at its height. In August I had been posted to Minehead as an instructor at a Battle School which had been formed to train platoon commanders on the moor. I was twenty-two at the time and had been brought up to foxhunting, having been blooded in 1925 by the great Pytchley huntsman Frank Freeman. Most of my hunting as a teenager had been in Yorkshire with the Bedale and Zetland when my father was stationed at Catterick, and I returned there as an officer in 1938 for the last pre-war hunting season when I had fifty-three days.

I had never been staghunting and knew nothing about it. So my first move on arrival at Minehead was to hire a horse from Joe Collings who ran a well-known livery stable in the old Tan Yard at Porlock. He came from a family of horse dealers who owned the horse auction, known as "The Horse Repository" at Exeter, which was run by his elder brother. Joe went to Porlock and established what became a thriving business hiring horses mostly for the staghounds. His son, Tony, who was a beautiful horseman, had attended a course with Jack Hance, a former army riding master, who had established an Equitation School in the Midlands. Tony had started to give riding lessons at Porlock, but as soon as war broke out he joined the North Somerset Yeomanry, and by the time I arrived was in Palestine with his regiment. His father Joe was a real old-fashioned job master, who produced a small blue roan mare for me, saying, "You will find she is just a piece of cake."

It was not a great day's hunting. After a turn round Acmead and Mill Hill we went into Culbone where we spent the rest of the day in local hunting. But I learnt one lesson. I was following the huntsman Alfred Lenthall, who pulled up to a trot as we approached what looked to me a lovely green piece of moor. So I cantered on, and the next thing I knew was the mare started floundering and rolled over on to her side dropping me into a bog. Fortunately no harm was done, and it taught me to follow the locals with care, and also that the moor was not all it seemed.

At the end of the day I asked the Master, Mrs Flo Hancock, mother of the Rev. Rex, the way back to Porlock. She said, "It is quite easy, but Judy Pilcher will be riding back that way. She will show you." So we were introduced, and I was not sorry as she was a very pretty girl, and I had noticed her on a thoroughbred horse at the top of the hunt. As we rode down the main road above Whitstones she pointed with her whip to a long grey house on the hill opposite and said, "That's where I live. Why don't you come in for a cup of tea?" Which, not surprisingly, I did. That day changed my life. Judy and I married the following year, and her home, Lynch on Exmoor, became our base. After the war I left the army and became a barrister and later a judge like her father, Sir Gonne (Toby) Pilcher. And I became an inveterate staghunter. Judy said afterwards that she had only asked me in to tea because her mother had told her to be nice to any soldier who was out hunting. But the consequence for both of us was dramatic.

Judy and I managed about twenty-five days hunting during the winter of 1940/41, mostly with the D&SS. I soon discovered that staghunting was a unique sport and that if you lived on Exmoor it was the thing to do. I also thought that foxhunting on Exmoor was a third rate sport, as the foxes did not run so far as the deer and there was no jumping. I always rode a Collings hireling while she had her own horse, which she looked after herself, as the groom at Lynch had been called up, although the cowman did the mucking out. Judy at the time was working as a land girl for Dick Clarke at West Luccombe

Major Eric Clegg, Lady Pilcher, Betty Rawle of Court Farm,
Porlock, and another, 1931

Farm. At that time the Joint Masters of the D&SS were Tommy and
Flo Hancock and Biddy Abbot, although Tommy was away in the
army, so Flo and Biddy were in charge. The Hancocks, from the well-
known West Country brewing family, lived at Rhyl Manor. Flo was
American and a considerable character. Years later, when she had
moved to Porlock and had been to Holy Communion at the Lynch
Chapel, she said to the Parson on leaving, with reference to the
Confession: "I don't find my sins at all intolerable." "Well you should,
Mrs Hancock," was his reply. Biddy Abbot was an even stronger
character, and if she had been a man would have been a splendid
divisional commander in wartime. She was a spinster who lived in
Dulverton near her sister Joyce. Their father had been a successful
solicitor in Bristol and they were connected with the Quaker Fry
family, makers of chocolate. From her youth Biddy had been devoted
to staghunting, about which she was extremely knowledgeable, and
to which she was very generous. On her death she left Hinam Farm

on the River Barle to the Badgworthy Land Company, which was the land-holding branch of the Hunt.

In 1940 the D&SS had just passed through what must have been a golden age. From 1919 to 1937 the Master had been Colonel Walter Wiggin from Warwickshire, who lived next to the kennels at Stockleigh Lodge in Exford. His huntsman had been the famous Ernest Bawden, who from 1916 to 1937 had shown the most wonderful sport and whose exploits had become legendary. He came from an Exmoor farming family. In 1940 the huntsman was Alfred Lenthall, first whipper-in to Ernest and no mean huntsman himself, with a vast knowledge of the deer and their habits. Unfortunately he suffered from poor health and retired in 1951, to be succeeded by Sidney Bazeley, who was also knowledgeable about the deer, and after ten years as huntsman became harbourer from 1972 to 1976. He was small and light and the best horseman I ever saw on the moor.

The harbourer was Hector Heywood, who lived and farmed at Cloutsham. Not only did he know the whereabouts of most of the deer on Exmoor, but he was also a skilled naturalist with an encyclo-paedic knowledge of all wildlife. He loved to go to Scotland during the rut in the Highlands, and was an intelligent and well educated man.

Judy and I were married on 23 August 1941 and a month to the day afterwards I left with my regiment for the Middle East. Although I returned a year later, having been wounded near Tobruk, I was posted to command a battery training for the invasion of France, where I landed in Normandy on 6 June 1944 ('D' Day), so there was not much time for hunting during the rest of the war. But hunting continued, supported by the Government who regarded venison as a valuable source of protein. The US Army used the North Forest of Exmoor as an artillery range when they entered the war in 1942. Hunting was allowed, but on firing days red flags were flown as a warning. The target area was Acmead, Larkbarrow (the farm was destroyed), and Mill Hill. The guns were in position at Webbers Post, and on the slopes of Dunkery. Things however did not always go according to plan, as appears from the following extract from Flo

Hancock's diary dated 21 September 1943, by permission of the Rev. Rex.

Meet, Wheddon Cross. Tamsie and I rode on from the Stables, & arrived to find a large field amongst whom was Edmund Myers, who when last out with us was Capt. & now a Brig. & a DSO. Also out our two new millionaire supporters, Towler of Stowey & Blakiston of Dulverton. Made myself known to former who seemed pleasant & very expensively turned out.

Stag harboured in N. Hawkswell. Tufters left for there while we took pack to wait at Dunk. Hill Gate, it being understood on no account were we to cross the Exford-Hawkcombe Hd. road, because of firing practise. On way to D.H. Gate met Post Officer who said there were guns at Webbers Post as well as just above Allercombe. Slightly shaken by this news, but decided if we cd. convey this to Alfred, he would not be taken unawares.

Hounds were soon heard running in Hannicombe & I made my first & unsuccessful attempt to meet with Alfred above Hannicombe.

Hounds ran within view below Dunk. H. G. & disappeared on to Codsend. We despatched Toby (Pilcher) & Jimmy (Taplin) to try and get in touch with Alfred, & the field were encouraged to spread out all along the fringe of Dunkery to keep the stag from crossing over the road to Hurdle Down.

The rain as usual began descending and loud explosions could be heard & shells seen exploding in the target area, while various members of the field had blood curdling tales of guns going off under their horses' noses coming on to the meet. I left Biddy & the Pack to canter along the Codsend fence & try to discover if Toby & Jimmy were carrying out their job & to my dismay soon heard hounds running up onto Exford Common & shortly after saw some going streaking across Hurdle Down with shells exploding away on Acmead, not far in front of the way they were running. A whistle then blew at the end of Codsend Lane & as I approached I could see Jimmy & Toby with Alfred arriving from the Kitnor Heath side in an awful state & Jimmy remarking he just couldn't get there in time to stop tufters. Alf. then turned his horse round, saying he was jolly well going to see where his best 7 couple got to & "come on Jimmy!" Down the road he galloped but not a hoof stirred except for 4 faithful ones the property of mystery. In a commanding tone the Joint yelled to the retreating figure, "You are not to risk your life Alfred", so we stuck to the road, turning right for Hawk. & soon met our first American soldier.

Alf. addressed him to ask for news of hounds, to be answered in deliberate tones by "I don't get you Buddy". At Black Myers X there were a mass of men & vehicles & a nasty cannon in full view. Here we managed to get news that hounds had been seen going away over Mill Hill & that the road fortunately was not closed to Hawk. Head. On arriving there we could see a vast encampment spread out below Oare Post & I began to lose some of the shivers up & down my back bone, as I felt no shells would drop short in that area by accident.

We made for Culbone, but all was quiet within & then dropped down Beggars Knap to Robbers Bridge, where ambulances were tucked safely in behind high banks, while above on the high ground those nasty menacing red flags were flying. An ambulance officer then told us they had heard hounds speak over in the direction of Oare, so on we went and soon to our unspeakable relief we distinctly heard them ourselves coming in from P. of Wales Bog direction, & quite quickly we got to them, hunting the line down behind Oare Manor. Such was my relief I secretly yearned to collect them then & there, but needless to say not so Alf. & on we persevered while incredulous friends popped out from field & house to make sure it really was hounds they were hearing & before long we were joined by Burge & Son, Nancekivell, & here & there a holiday male & female.

Hounds were having a difficult job to puzzle out the line in the water, Alf. casting all the way down to Brendon, but we got information here & there & learned a single hound was on well ahead. This proved our Waterloo, as the deer had not been able to lie up & news eventually reached us that a hound was seen taking a line down to the beach between Yenworthy & Glenthorne. The following day a telephone message reached Alf. that Heedless was shut up at Glenthorne.

I then began to wonder if our thrills were over for the day, or if more

Miss Biddy Abbot sending for the pack with Ralph Slocombe harbourer, 1950.

incidents were in store on the homeward way, & my vertebrae would begin to prick once again, but except for the screaming of the shells being fired over our heads from the direction of Leigh Hill which we could see landing on Manor Allotment & which incidentally we timed as taking 14 seconds from the firing to the exploding and which Alfred, (to my great admiration!) worked out as really only taking 8 seconds, as it took 4 seconds for sound to reach our ears. We had a peaceful trek home, first stopping in at Oare for a very welcome drink, & to get a telephone message back to Biddy at the Stables whom I knew would be horribly worried, for she would get all sorts of messages I felt sure from members of the field as to what had happened.

We also halted at Jack Wollacot's to see the head of the stag he had found badly wounded and had killed in one of his fields the previous week. I could not gather whether it was by shell or rifle bullets, but think probably the latter "deer shooting" being hunting in the U.S.A.

CHAPTER II

The Wild Red Deer

EXMOOR is practically the only place in England which supports a herd of wild red deer. The exact number is debateable but is, according to the latest count, probably about 3,000 within the area of the Exmoor National Park, showing a slight increase over the years. What is not in dispute is that the herd is the healthiest in the United Kingdom. Unlike Dartmoor, where the deer were slaughtered in the 19th Century by the farmers, the deer on Exmoor have been encouraged and managed by the Hunt, the Devon & Somerset Staghounds, although in the middle of the 19th Century hunting was stopped and the deer were almost exterminated. When it resumed the herd flourished under the management of the Hunt. Farmers were discouraged from shooting deer, and to do so was regarded as akin to homicide. For many years the deer were lassooed and their throats cut at the end of a hunt, and in France to this day they are killed with a sword. But in this country, at least from the end of the Great War, deer have been shot at the end of a hunt. An experienced local farmer uses a sawn-off shotgun attached to his saddle, and when the deer stands at bay it is shot at point blank range. It is either killed or escapes. In addition all members of the Hunt staff carry humane killers in case the gun is not available at the end of the hunt. The Hunt also provides a valuable service by humanely despatching "casualties" which in the nineties amounted to as many as 50 deer in a year. These were injured deer, some as a result of motor accidents and others the result of shooting. Some of the injuries were horrific, and many deer became gangrenous and died in agony after many days, if they were not located by the Hunt. In addition the Hunt killed about 100 deer during the hunting season. Until the Deer Act 1963 there were also about three "deer drives" every season, when a covert was ringed by guns, and a few hounds were put in to move the deer. The purpose of this was to cull the hinds, whose numbers need to be limited if the herd is to be properly managed and damage reduced. If there are too many hinds stags will cover their daughters, thus reducing the strength of the herd.

In 2004 hunting was banned by the Hunting Act, although there were certain exemptions which have enabled the D&SS to keep going until 2008 in a limited way. The following account was written before the ban was imposed, and describes how staghunting was conducted during the time that I took part in it. It is taken from my memoirs, *Sword & Wig.*

The stag-hunting season revolves round the annual life cycle of the deer. On Exmoor the three lowest points on a stag's horns are called his "rights" – brow, bay and tray. As the stag grows older he will have more and longer points "on top", so that a twelve pointer or Royal on Exmoor is described as having all his rights and three on top. Many of the older stags have a fine spread of antlers and then the head starts to decline as the stag "goes back". The stags drop their horns in April when hunting stops and grow new horns during the summer, suffering a good deal of discomfort in the process. The nascent horns are covered with a protective layer of "velvet", which falls away in August when stag-hunting starts and the big stags which are past their prime or "going back" are hunted until the rut in late October. The hunt employs a harbourer, always a local with knowledge of the deer, and often an experienced naturalist who, in conjunction with the local farmer, harbours a "warrantable" stag the night before hunting. Initially the harbourer tracks or "slots" the deer, the stag's foot being called a slot. The harbourer can tell from the slot mark not only the sex but also the age of the deer, and the huntsman will often slot the deer during a hunt when it has joined other deer so as to keep the hounds on the hunted deer. Early next morning the harbourer watches the stag move out from the covert to his

A hunted stag coming past the field on Anstey Common

grazing ground where he settles, usually in a bunch of ferns. At that time of year they are amazingly difficult to see despite their size and it was a great treat to be allowed to go out with the harbourer before hunting. The harbourers notice everything in the countryside, the movement of pigeons or sheep, the call of a jay and other signs all of which can point to the presence of deer. The harbourer goes to the meet, tells the huntsman where the stag is lying and the tufters (about four couple of experienced hounds) are drawn, while the rest of the pack is kennelled, usually nowadays in the hound van. The tufters rouse the stag and then, when it is clear of the woods and other deer, the tufters are stopped and the pack laid on. The tufting can often take up to two hours and is watched by the mounted field and crowds of foot followers from some point of vantage. Nothing is more exciting than the laying on of the pack, which is brought up by a whipper-in and the second horsemen. The hunt servants change horses, the huntsman blows his horn, the hounds settle to the line and start to give tongue and everyone tightens their girths and sits down to ride as hard as they can over the heather. There is a great sense of urgency from the moment the pack arrives. It usually takes about twenty minutes from the time the tufters are stopped until the time the pack is laid on, so that the stag is given that amount of law.

When the rut starts stag-hunting stops, as the stags become exhausted by their labours and lose condition. They sometimes travel miles in search of a bunch of hinds. The rut is the time to see the deer, as they are on the move when the big stags are collecting their hinds. The best time to see them is in the evening when the stags roar or "bell", an eerie sound almost like the roar of a lion. I once saw a cheeky young stag cover a hind while his lord and master was leading the hinds down into a combe in the gloaming. When the rut is over, hind-hunting starts. The hinds will have dropped their calves in June, so that they are weaned by November and are hunted until the end of February, although by then many will be pregnant, 75% of the growth of the foetus takes place in the last six weeks, so the foetus is tiny while the hinds are being hunted.

The technique of hind-hunting is quite different from stag-hunting. After the rut the stags leave their hinds (they are not good fathers) and the hinds congregate into herds of thirty or more. The tufters are laid straight on to a herd and the hunt servants and some young farmers try to cut out one or more hinds. The tufters may divide and settle onto one or two or even three single hinds. This is all confusing to the novice follower, who has to decide which group to follow often in mist and the moor riding wet and treacherous. The tufters are not stopped and the pack is laid on when the opportunity arises. This requires great skill and control by the hunt servants. Ideally, when one hind is killed, the pack will be laid on to another which has been hunted by perhaps a couple or more tufters. The primary purpose of hind-hunting is to cull the maximum number of hinds. Deer are herd animals and, unlike stags which usually run straight, hinds tend to run in large circles in an attempt to return to the herd.

Spring stag-hunting starts in early March and continues until the end of April. This is the best time for hunting on Exmoor and many people from "up-country" bring their horses down after they have stopped fox-hunting, so that there are often meets of up to three hundred riders with the staghounds. In the spring the younger stags and those with mis-shapen heads are hunted. The run of a stag is fairly predictable, although it has changed over the years with the fencing of parts of Exmoor. Deer will fly over fences while being hunted, but while grazing they tend not to do so. They prefer to keep to the high ground where the going is good, so it is best for the rider to keep on the high ground, although Judy liked to follow as close to the hounds as she could. The autumn stags usually make a point where there are likely to be other deer, but the spring stags are more unpredictable and often provide great hunts. The best day's stag-hunting I ever had was on 25th April 1957 when we ran from Hawkridge near Dulverton straight over the moor to near Lynmouth when hounds were stopped as they were getting close to the town. It was a seventeen-mile point all over open country, and lasted two-and-a-half hours from the time the pack was laid on. We only crossed three roads. I rode Lincoln Lad, an ex-racehourse with doubtful legs and a horrible trick of dropping his shoulder, whipping round and putting you on the ground. But that day he excelled himself and we were with hounds all the way.

A blood horse is required on Exmoor if one is to keep anywhere near hounds when they run, preferably one with short legs as a big long-striding horse tends to knock its legs on the rough ground in the river valleys and combes. The ideal was Judy's Collough, brought over for her from Ireland by Tony Collings at the price of £90. Collough was a 15-hand chestnut mare by Sun King by Hyperion, winner of the Triple Crown. Like her august grandsire she had lop ears and moved like a machine with bottomless stamina. She also pulled like a train. Once, climbing up Hangley Cleeve in the middle of a long hunt when all the horses were reduced to a walk by the steep gradient, Collough and Judy went bounding up and when they reached the top Collough threw a buck just to show how she felt. One year in the fifties, when Willy, our groom, was away with my horse at the Bar point-to-point, the children persuaded Judy to run Collough in the hunt race at the Staghounds' point-to-point. By that time, after a hard season, Collough had been turned out to grass, so Judy caught her in, fed her, groomed her and put up Norman Williams, son of a neighbouring farmer, to ride her. She won, never being headed all the way. She would stick her neck out and just go, although she had little regard for the obstacles, and Norman did well to remain in the saddle. Thereafter she won several point-to-points until she finally decided she had had enough of racing and returned to the hunting field.

Deer are destructive animals. They will go into a field of roots and take a bite out of every swede or turnip, throwing them over their shoulders in disdain. The farmers accept this level of damage only because the overwhelming majority of them support stag-hunting. On Dartmoor, where the deer have never been hunted, the red deer are now practically extinct having been slaughtered by the farmers. But the Exmoor hill farmers preserve the deer, because their whole life-style revolves around hunting. "No hunting, no deer" is not just a slogan. It is accepted as true by all independent observers. The hill farmers are the true aristocracy of Exmoor, their families having farmed there for generations. It is even now a hard and lonely life, especially in the winter, and the hunt provides the only relaxation and opportunity to socialise. Many of the hill farming families inter-marry, since it is difficult for someone not brought up on the moor to adapt to the peculiar way of life. The great 18th century prosperity did not extend to Exmoor, so apart from a few large houses near Dulverton, such as Pixton Park, there were few houses of any size on the moor. There were the two big estates owned by the Fortescues and Aclands and their yeomen tenants and shepherds. It was not until this century (20th Century) that, attracted by the stag-hunting and helped by the railway, people with money started to build houses and settle on Exmoor. Until the second world war the hill farmers suffered from the general agricultural depression but still went hunting on their Exmoor shepherding ponies, their feet almost touching the ground. During and after the war, however, with the great revival of agriculture, many of the tenants bought their farms at knockdown prices and benefited from the general prosperity of farming. Now they ride thoroughbred horses which their sons and daughters point-to-point; and the latter look like princesses and are as well mounted.

The technique of hunting staghounds is also different from that of foxhounds. The "all round the hat" cast, as advocated by the famous 19th-Century huntsman Tom Smith in his book *Diary of a Huntsman* (1838), which seeks to make good all the ground round the point where the hounds gave up the scent, is not generally followed. The scent of deer is generally stronger than that of foxes, and more reliance is placed on the likely run of the deer, which is more predictable. Deer will often run for water and then run up or down the numerous rivers and streams on Exmoor. Much of the casting therefore takes place along the rivers and on their banks, and requires a great deal of skill. The decision, on reaching a river, whether to cast up or downstream is a vital one, and I have known very long casts along the waters before the line is recovered.

Staghunting is also less competitive among its followers than foxhunting. There is more room and fewer enclosures, and the importance of a "good start" is not so great. And of course there is no jumping, so no queuing at fences and fewer gateways. The hounds do not run with such a good head as foxhounds, nor do they have the cry. It was not until after the Great War that the Staghounds bred their own hounds. Until then they drafted hounds in from packs of foxhounds. The hounds are now bred by the Master Maurice Scott, assisted by the huntsman Donald Summersgill. Since the Hunting Act fewer hounds have been bred, and many have been loaned to packs in France, where staghunting still flourishes. During the time that I was hunting however, the breeding of hounds was active and the puppy walkers were valuable supporters of the Hunt. In order to avoid inbreeding, stallion hounds were used from outside the country, notably the Wynnstay and Brocklesbury. Old English foxhounds were the preferred strain. Modern foxhounds as exemplified by the Exmoor were found unsuitable, as they were bred to hunt foxes and would not settle to deer. The ideal staghound is rather smaller than the modern foxhound but more stocky and tougher. Considerable stamina is required, as the hunts can be long, lasting for several hours. In the 19th Century there was no hunting in the winter because the waters were considered too cold for the hounds. I found myself more physically tired after a day's staghunting than I ever was foxhunting. In a normal lowland hunting country one can sit "at ease" for much of the time, only riding at the fences. But on Exmoor one has to be riding all the time, since the moor is rough, with many ditches and holes in the ground which the horse can put his foot in and stumble.

Part of the pleasure of hunting on Exmoor is the beauty of the country and its variety during the year. There is the contrast between the wooded combes, the green "in-bye fields", and the heather moorland behind. In the winter it is dark and forbidding, with the rain sometimes driven horizontally by the wind, so that it is difficult to stay on one's horse. But even then there are beautiful clear days with the light changing as the clouds scud across the sky. Then in the spring the moor comes alive when the ferns begin to peep, until it reaches its full glory when the heather comes out in August. Finally in the autumn the bracken turns red and then yellow, and the colours are superb.

This description of staghunting is no longer possible today since the passing of the Hunting Act. The old skills of tufting and laying on the pack are no longer possible since only two hounds are allowed. So the traditional management of the herd of wild red deer by the Hunt, which has been so successful, is threatened. Let us hope for the benefit of the deer that it will be able to be resumed.

CHAPTER III

The Murphy and Nancekivell Years
1958-1974

F OR THE FIRST ten years after the war there were a number of changes of masterships between 1951 and 1955, the country being hunted by the Committee with Mrs Ned Lloyd and H.P. Hewett as acting Masters, followed by Colonel Murphy and Mrs

H.P. Hewett and Mrs Violet Lloyd-Masters
on behalf of the Committee, 1952

25

Sidney Bazeley leading the field, mid 1950s

Ralph Slocombe (harbourer) and Mrs Lloyd, 1953

Denis Cox. All these people played a large part in the administration of the D&SS. Mrs Ned Lloyd's husband, who had lost an arm in the Great War, had been Secretary from 1923 until 1929. They lived at Pitsworthy and their son Dick was Secretary from 1947 to 1952. On his return from National Service in India in 1947, Dick became farm manager to Sir Bernard Waley-Cohen, later Lord Mayor of London, and owner of the Honeymead Estate. Bernard succeeded Earl Fortescue as Chairman of the Hunt Committee in 1953, ably

Hector Heywood, Sidney Bazeley and Harry Onions
(father of Rosemary Pile), late 1950s

assisted by Dick Lloyd, who became Vice Chairman in 1974. Together
they ran the Hunt until 1985 when Bernard retired to be succeeded
by Dick.

It was a perfect combination. Bernard was not only an astute
businessman, but also had contacts in political circles in London,

which became increasingly important during the long campaign to ban hunting, in which staghunting was very much in the front line. Bernard, despite his size and girth, was a first class horseman. One year he won the Hunt Race at the D&SS point-to-point on his good horse Benelux. I was in the Winners Enclosure with his wife Joyce when he came out from the weighing tent, saying, "I made the weight all right." At that moment the loudspeaker announced, "Winner weighed in 3 stone overweight." Dick probably knew more about staghunting than anyone on Exmoor after the war. He knew every inch of the country and all the farmers. He had as much ability as his twin brother Pat, who became a Master of Wine and chief buyer for one of the largest wine merchants in the country. But he chose to devote his life to Exmoor and staghunting.

H.P. Hewett had spent his life working for the Government Woods and Forests Department in Burma. But his roots were on Exmoor and his brother, known as "Sunset Douglas" because of the colour of his face, lived at Larkbarrow Farm, which was destroyed by American artillery during the Second World War. They were both batchelors and devoted to staghunting, and on his retirement H.P. Hewett built Whithill at Wootton Courtenay, where he lived until his death. Norah Cox was married to Denis Cox, who had been in the RAF during the Great War and had injured his head when his aircraft had crashed. They owned the White Horse Hotel and stables at Exford, and became Joint Masters of the Staghounds from 1955 to 1957, Norah having been acting Master for the Committee the previous two years, and continued as sole Master until 1958. Norah was the daughter of Colonel Heath, a Lancashire mill owner and Chairman of the Tarporley Hunt Club in Cheshire. He used to bring Norah and his other daughter, Peggy, to Exmoor for the staghunting. Norah married Denis Cox and Peggy married Ernest Yandle of Riphay Barton near Dulverton, who was closely involved with the Tiverton Staghounds. Their son is Tom Yandle, the present Chairman of the D&SS and a great figure on Exmoor. The other key figure in the immediate post-war years was Colonel Michael Murphy. He had served in the Indian Cavalry before the Second World War, and

Tom Yandle of Riphay Barton, Chairman of the Hunt Committee, the
Master of Deerhounds Association and the Badgworthy Land Company.
Born and bred on Exmoor; a successful farmer and former High Sheriff
of Somerset. He and his wife Margaret keep open house at Riphay.

had become Chief of Intelligence Staff at the Headquarters of
General Montgomery. There is a photograph of him standing beside
Monty at the signing of the German surrender at Luneburg in 1945.
Soon after the war Michael and his wife bought Monkham House in
Exford, and from 1952 to 1958 he was Secretary of the D&SS. From
1958 to 1963 he was sole Master of the D&SS. Unlike the others I
have mentioned, Michael was not brought up on Exmoor. But he was
a highly intelligent man who took a great deal of trouble to learn the
habits of the deer and the peculiarities of staghunting. He was a heavy
smoker and used to sit chain smoking while watching the tufters. He
became much respected on Exmoor.

In 1963 Michael resigned, and was succeeded by Nigel Hambro
and Bob Nancekivell, for a year on behalf of the Committee and then,
until 1969, as Masters in their own right. Nigel Hambro was from the
well-known banking family, but preferred living and farming at

Presentation by Sir Bernard Waley-Cohen of a picture
to Colonel Murphy on his retirement as Master, April 1963.
Mrs Murphy is also in the photograph.

Withypool to working in the City of London. He was a cheerful and agreeable Master, and any deficiency in his knowledge of staghunting was more than made up by his Joint Master, Bob Nancekivell, who was a builder from Lynton. But all his life he had been a keen staghunter with wide knowledge of the moor. When he was a young man he was befriended by Sir Brian Mountain of the Eagle Star Insurance, who owned the Oare Manor Estate. Sir Brian sold the Manor House and Cloud Farm to Bob, who promptly sold the Manor for more money than he had paid for the whole estate. Thereafter he lived and farmed at Cloud, although he was responsible for rebuilding Lynmouth after the disastrous floods of 1952.

Walter Perry and Bob Nancekivell, 1960s

This made his fortune, and enabled him to be Master of the Staghounds. He was a big man in every way, known as "the King of the Forest", and one of the best men to go across the moor I ever saw. He always rode with a bitless bridle or hackamore and his horses went brilliantly for him. No day was too long, although he was a diabetic. But he was not always very tactful with the press, at a time when the Staghounds were in the full glare of publicity. So Bernard and I redrafted the Mastership Agreement adding a clause which provided that Bob should not speak to the press and should refer all inquiries to the British Field Sports Society. I remember the drafting was done at Rules Restaurant at Covent Garden in London during an excellent dinner, starting with smoked royal sturgeon.

Sidney Bazeley was the last huntsman to have worked under Ernest Bawden. Sidney was a beautiful horseman. He was a lightweight so could ride small active horses and it was a delight to see him cross the moor, sitting easily in the saddle. And, having whipped-in to Ernest Bawden, he was no mean huntsman. After he retired as

Sir Robin and Lady Dunn with Dick Carpendale,
Hon Secretary, in the background, 1970

huntsman he became harbourer for several years, where his knowledge of the deer paid dividends. He was followed by Bill Lock, who only stayed for two years before leaving to go to foxhounds. His successor was Walter Perry, who had been groom to Sir Bernard Waley-Cohen at Honeymead. He was heavier than previous huntsmen and thus more difficult to mount. He was huntsman from 1963 to 1971 and I remember some good hunts with him. He was very popular with the farmers, and had their full support, which is important for a huntsman. From my point of view I think he lifted his hounds too often. But that is common with staghounds, and perhaps it was because of my foxhunting background that I preferred to see hounds being allowed to run on, on their own. Walter went on to hunt the Quantock Staghounds, where he was very popular.

Waiting for the pack, Nutscale: Joyce Lady Waley-Cohen, Dennis Boyles, Judy Lady Dunn, Sir Robin Dunn and Peter Cox (on foot with back to camera)

In 1971 Bob Nancekivell engaged Dennis Boyles as huntsman, who stayed for twenty years. He was already an experienced Hunt servant, having started as a second horseman with the D&SS. He had been sacked by Mrs Lloyd and H.P. Hewett for taking the pack to the wrong place, and worked for various packs of foxhounds up the country, including whipping in to the Belvoir and hunting hounds elsewhere. Over a long period he showed sport of a high standard and killed more deer than had ever been killed hunting on Exmoor before. But as he grew older he became increasingly impatient with his horses and less inclined to leave the shelter of the woodlands during the winter. During this time there were also some knowlegeable harbourers, including Ralph Slocombe, who had worked in the kennels with Ernest Bawden, Bill Harding, Donald Pile and Edgar Webber, who farmed one of the Badgworthy Land Company farms at Walland, near Wheddon Cross.

After the war Judy and I hunted as much as we could. I left the army in 1948 and went to the Bar. Until 1962, when I became a QC, I was too busy building up my practice in London to be able to hunt

Peter Cox and Dennis Boyles on Nutscale

much at weekends, although the stables were running at Lynch and we each kept a horse there. But I always spent a month at Lynch in August and September, and also ten days or a fortnight at Christmas and Easter. In those days before horseboxes we hunted mostly on the north side of the moor. But it was always said at Lynch, "Never miss a meet at Yarde Down". So on 20 September 1947 we went to the "Barnstaple Fair" meet, which took place every year to coincide with the Fair. I was short of a horse so Leslie Scott of East Lynch Farm lent me a good point-to-point horse called Orel. Judy rode her Blagdon who, although not thoroughbred, was quite fast enough even to keep up with the D&SS bitch pack running on a good scent. We sent the horses on to Simonsbath the night before and hacked on to Yarde Down in the morning. We found in Wort Wood in the Bray valley at about 11.45, the stag running straight up over Whitefield Down, by Moles Chamber, over the Challacombe road at Driver and across the edge of the Chains. He then crossed Cheriton Ridge, Farley Water, over the Brendon Road, across Badgworthy to Mill Hill, and at

Crossing the water: Dennis Boyles on the River Barle with hounds

Dennis Boyles passing Larkbarrow

1.15pm we passed the AA Box on the A39 road at the top of the Porlock toll road. There was no check and hounds did not have to be touched all the way. They ran with a great cry down Worthy Combe and killed on the beach at Porlock Weir. A wonderful hunt which brought us to within a few miles of Lynch.

It was during this period that the organisation of the D&SS was developed. Very soon after the war Tony Collings, who was always full of ideas and had set up his very successful Equitation Centre at Porlock, suggested to the Hunt Committee that staghunting should be publicised nationally so as to encourage people to come and spend money on Exmoor. His argument was that skiing had become fashionable because of good marketing. Because no-one was allowed to take more than £25 out of the country due to the strict Exchange Control laws, fewer people were going abroad, and this was an opportunity to make staghunting fashionable. This view was strongly opposed by Lord Fortescue, the Chairman of the Committee. He said that it was very dangerous for a Hunt to rely on outside sources of finance, whether from rich benefactors who did not live in the country, or from visitors. He insisted that the bulk of the revenue should come from within the country and that there were many people such as hoteliers, garage owners, feed merchants and others who benefited financially from the Hunt and that they should be encouraged to support it. So the Hunt Club was formed. It was one of the first, if not the first, Hunt Club in the country, and it was very active in fund-raising. John Keep was the first Chairman. He lived at Marsh House and was a keen staghunter. His wife always followed in the car and was ready with hot drinks and other sustenance at the end of the day. One of our children once said, "Why can't we have a nice mother like little Mrs Keep?" One of the most successful ventures was the sheep scheme. It was started by the Hunt buying a number of lambs and farming them out with farmers, who did not charge for their keep. When they were sold the money was paid to the Hunt, part of it being used to buy more sheep and part given to Hunt funds. Over the years a substantial sum was accumulated. My father-in-law started a football pool, which involved a good deal of organization since there were agents in each parish who collected the cash and distributed the prizes. And there were the progressive whist drives in all the villages. After some years the Hunt Supporters Club was formed, which was aimed at the younger supporters and organised for many years by Tom Yandle's son Tim at Riphay Barton. The result of all this fundraising was that, whereas in 1928 the Master's guarantee was £3,000, by 2003, the year before the Hunting Act, it was £163,396. The Hunt Club paid £35,000, the Hunt Supporters Club £17,500 and the Sheep Account stood at £10,828. Subscriptions stood at £114,289, Caps £41,253 and Field Money £32,236. So the finances of the D&SS were in a robust state thanks to the foresight of those in charge of the Hunt immediately after the war.

Another substantial source of income over the years has been the point-to-point. Before the Second World War there had only been one point-to-point, at Honeymead in 1939. But the course had been shrouded in fog, so after the war it was decided to hold a meeting on the Dunster Lawns, by permission of Mr Geoffrey Luttrell. But this was not a success; the course was flat and uninteresting, and it was decided to move to Holnicote, by then owned by the National Trust, who welcomed the idea. The prime movers in this were my father-in-law, Toby Pilcher, and Leslie Scott of East Lynch Farm, both of whom had been successful point-to-point riders before the war. The original plan had been that the course should have one large circuit crossing the Pile's Mill lane and going up to Horridge Wood, and then back over the lane below Ebbs Hill on to the flat fields near Holnicote House. But the police objected to two crossings of the public lane, so it was decided to confine the course to the fields between the A39 and the Pile's Mill lane. In order to achieve a course of three miles, two and a half circuits were necessary. All the same, the course was full of interest, there being a water jump over the River Aller and a "drop" fence just beyond the winning post. It was decided that a late date was likely to attract more spectators than an early one, although the entries might be adversely affected. So the first Saturday in May was fixed. My father-in-law was Chairman and Dick Lloyd Secretary of the Point-to-Point Committee for many years. Leslie Scott was Clerk of the Course. The point-to-point was a huge success, with large crowds coming to Holnicote every year. The fields were never very big, as it was near the end of the point-to-point season and some horses were lame or had had enough for the season. But the crowds continued to come, partly because of the beauty of the country round the course, and the views from it. The whole ambience was delightful and it was a lovely place for a picnic, with the racing an added attraction. The paddock was near the famous Gladstone Oak, which had been planted in 1877 to mark a visit by the then Prime Minister to Sir Thomas Acland MP at Holnicote House.

My father-in-law was succeeded as Chairman by Colonel Jamie Crawford, owner of the famous riding school at Porlock, from whom I took over in the 1980s. Although the lower part of the course tended to be wet even in May, the meeting only once had to be cancelled due to bad weather. The course was popular with point-to-point owners and riders. Bertie Hill, later winner of an Olympic Gold Medal, was a frequent rider, as was John Daniel from the Berkeley, who rode the horses of Lucy Jones, a very successful owner. After I handed the Chairmanship over to Mick Palmer of Court Place, Porlock, it was decided to move the course to East Luccombe Farm, where the going was considered better, with better viewing for spectators. But the course has not the charm of the old course at Holnicote, and I do not believe it is so popular with spectators. However, in 2003 the point-to-point contributed £6,500 to Hunt funds.

A further substantial contribution to the Hunt finances is made by the car caps. These are collected by dedicated car cappers who go to the meets in all weathers to take voluntary payments from the drivers.

The profits from the Exford Show also go to the Hunt. This is a popular event which includes not only the traditional classes for hunters and ponies, but also a special ring for the Exmoor Pony Society. The staghounds are always shown in the ring and receive a great welcome from the crowd. The Show is held in August on the Wednesday before the Opening Meet. The "in hand" classes have always been particularly strong at Exford.

Another important adjunct of the Hunt is the Pony Club, although staghunting is not really suitable for young children until they are old enough to ride a galloping pony which can keep up with hounds. After the war Tony Collings suggested that, instead of having separate Pony Clubs for each of the packs of foxhounds, there should be one for the whole of Exmoor run by the D&SS, and my mother-in-law Lady Pilcher became the first District Commissioner. The club flourished, and for the first time children were taught to ride properly. One farmer's wife, in introducing her son, said to Lady Pilcher: "You'll teach him manners, won't you?"

One of the most popular events in the 1950s was the annual Pony Club dance held during the Christmas holidays at Stenner's Restaurant in Minehead. The grown-ups wore evening hunt coats and the ladies their ball dresses, and they enjoyed the evening as much as the children as plenty of alcohol was available. At the end the whole party went out into the street, whatever the weather (there sometimes being snow on the ground), and danced the conger up and down the Parade, led by Johnnie Attwater dressed up as a Highland piper. Johnnie, who lived with his wife and two daughters at Periton House near Minehead, was an extraordinary character. He spent most of the summer in a hut he had built on a piece of land he owned near Luccombe Allers on the moor below Robin How, and which he called "Stag Hall". He was a keen staghunter, always riding a pony, and the only person I know who jumped the stone, faced banks instead of going through gates. But he did not ride over the bank, rather dismounting and driving the pony over, then following on foot and remounting the other side. Sadly Johnnie died recently.

Another Exmoor character at that time was Colonel Guy Jackson, who used to bring his daughter Charmian to the Pony Club parties. She has been Master of the Warwickshire for several years, but still hunts with the D&SS in the Spring. Guy was brought up in Warwickshire, where he was Master of the North Warwickshire before the war. But he also used to come staghunting on Exmoor, and in 1938/39 was field master with my father-in-law. He was in the Warwickshire Yeomanry, which he commanded at the Battle of El Alamein when he was awarded the DSO, and proved himself a born leader. Later in the war his regiment was in Italy, and after one battle Guy and some others went partridge shooting. Walking through a wood, Guy stepped on an anti-personnel mine and blew off his foot. He then put down the other foot which was also blown off by a mine. Fortunately it was only necessary to amputate his legs below the knee, so that he could be fitted with metal legs which enabled him to walk, ride and hunt. The physical effort must have been considerable, however, although it did not stop him hunting two or three days a week.

After the war Guy moved to Exmoor and bought Exe Cleave in Exford, becoming a very successful Master of the Exmoor Foxhounds. He once said that he went to every sheep auction (in those days these were held regularly at Exford and Yarde Down, as well as those now at Cutcombe and Blackmoor Gate), since that was the place where all the business was done on Exmoor, and where you learned what was happening in the farming world. But he continued to go staghunting. One day Judy was out with our son Allan, who was about 12 at the time. She was riding a thoroughbred and he a very hot pony. As they crossed the road by the Chetsford bridge Guy had a fall at the bottom of the track leading up to Almsworthy Common. Judy caught his horse, and then dismounted to help Guy, giving her horse to Allan to hold. Guy was a big heavy man and she had a considerable struggle to get him back into the saddle, while he was shouting, "Push woman – push!" All this time Allan's pony was jumping about and Judy's horse was whirling round with Allan doing his best to hold the rein. Eventually Guy was settled into his seat and picked up his stirrups. He clapped his spurs into the horse and cantered off up the track without a word of thanks or even a wave to Judy, who had some difficulty in getting on to her own horse, which was keen to follow Guy. However she so much admired Guy that she made no complaint, saying, "Oh well, I expect he was keen to get to hounds." Sadly Guy died of a heart attack, no doubt brought on by his efforts to keep moving.

My mother-in-law was succeeded as District Commissioner by Mrs Valerie Welchman of Wootton Courtenay. For many years the District Commissioner was Mrs Hazel Leeves of Picked Stones and Selworthy, and the current DC is Mrs Bella Capel of Wootton Courtenay.

Over the years the Branch has been very successful in competitions in most of the disciplines organised by the Pony Club at national level. In recent years this has been particularly so in the Pony Club games, where the team has been trained by Bella Capel. Many regular followers of the Staghounds started riding with the Pony Club.

CHAPTER IV

The Harding and Robinson Years
1974-1987

AFTER Denis Cox died his wife Norah married Norman Harding, who farmed at Burrough, near Timberscombe. Having already been Master in the fifties, Norah again took on the mastership on her own for two seasons, from 1974 to 1976, when she

Norah Harding, Maurice Scott, Mike Robinson, Jack Dallyn (harbourer) and Dennis Boyles

Norah Cox and Bob Nancekivell, about 1980

Tessa White and her mother, Wynn Lloyd, 1970s

was joined by Mike Robinson. Mike was a dentist in Minehead who had moved down from the north with his parents and sister, who worked with him in the surgery. They bought Hacketty Way in Porlock and Mike soon started hunting with the Staghounds. He was very well mounted and obviously had a good eye for a horse. In 1976 he joined Norah in the mastership, and they remained together until 1981, when they were joined by Maurice Scott who had been harbourer with Donald Pile since 1976. Mike was cheerful and made everyone feel welcome in the hunting field, and he and Norah, with Dennis Boyles, showed good sport over the years. One day a barrister friend of mine was riding back from hunting with a hill farmer, who asked him what he did for a living. When he said he was a barrister the farmer said, "Oh! A barrister? You might be Master of the Staghounds one day. We've got a dentist now." From 1977 to 1989

Moving off from Cloutsham Opening Meet

Donald Pile (harbourer) and Peter Cox (Hon Secretary),
Cloutsham, 1981

Norah's son Peter became Secretary, and was a great help to Norah in the field. Norah really devoted her life and much of her fortune to staghunting, and was a very popular figure, especially among the farmers. When she had been younger Norah had been one of the best women to go across the moor – with Dick Lloyd's wife, Wynn, and Judy. But as she grew older she became more circumspect, although she was never far from the action and always in control.

By this time I was a member of the Hunt Committee, my father-in-law Toby Pilcher having retired as Vice Chairman in 1953. He was also Chairman of the Committee of the Exmoor Foxhounds. The Hunt Committee consisted of twelve members in addition to the Chairman and Vice Chairman. It was a self-electing body with four members standing down each year for a year, so as to give the opportunity for change, although this was seldom exercised. The retirement age was 70. The Committee was supposed to consist of a mixture of

*Walner Robins of
Selworthy Farm,
Hon Secretary (later
Master and Huntsman,
Quantock Staghounds),
1974*

farmers and subscribers, though as the years passed the farmers became predominant. A very different situation from the pre-war and immediate post-war years. I remember Toby Pilcher returning from a meeting soon after the war, laughing and telling us that during a discussion of some topic Lord Fortescue, who was then Chairman, had said, "I've heard what the gentlemen have to say about this. Now I'd like to hear from the farmers"! I cannot imagine such a remark being made during my time on the Committee, when the farmers were not slow to express their views. In any event, by 1980 the only non-farmers on the Committee, apart from myself, were Stephen Waley-Cohen and Sir Robert Thompson, who lived in Winsford and had had a distinguished career in the Colonial Service, culminating in his being Chief of Staff to General Templer during the emergency in Malaya. He was regarded as an expert on counter-terrorism, and had been consulted by President Nixon as to the situation in Vietnam.

My primary job on the Committee was to act as honorary legal adviser, which became more important as the League Against Cruel Sports became more active. Staghunting had been a prime target for the animal rights movement since the Great War. Fred Beadle, a rich industrialist who lived at Stowey on the Brendons and farmed there and at Beasley, realised that if each sport tried to defend itself individually it was likely that each would be defeated individually. What we needed, he thought, was a blanket organisation to defend all field sports. So, at his instigation and with his support, the British Field Sports Society was formed, with its headquarters in London. For many years the Society kept a low profile, although a great deal of work was done behind the scenes in the corridors of power at Westminster, and many private members' bills seeking to ban hunting were defeated in the House of Commons with the support of the Society led by Marcus (now Lord) Kimball. The Society's parliamentary contacts were excellent, and it also provided help on public relations and legal issues. But no real attempt was made to enlist the hearts and minds of the general public in support of hunting, in particular staghunting, which was looked at askance by many foxhunting people, largely through ignorance because they thought, wrongly, that the deer were "pulled down" by the hounds instead of being shot at the end of the hunt. So the Society concentrated on the defensive strategy of damage limitation, seeking to explain and excuse the increasing number of "incidents" which the press delighted in publicising. On the other hand our opponents, the League Against Cruel Sports, although with a comparatively small membership, was very active and effective in its public relations, lobbying Members of Parliament and establishing good relations especially with the popular press. It is however significant that four of its former directors have changed sides; one actively supports the Middle Way movement which seeks to repeal the existing ban and replace it with a system of licensed hunting.

A particularly damaging incident was "the stag on the roof" in 1987. A hunted stag ran down the steep side of Hawkcombe, just above Porlock, on to the roof of a house which had been built close to the steep bank. The stag just stepped on to it and stood there. It was photographed by a passer-by who sent the photograph to the League Against Cruel Sports. It was widely published in the press under such headlines as "Terrified stag seeks refuge on roof of house".

Although the BFSS was quick to explain the true situation, the damage had been done.

During the 1970s the League followed a policy of buying parcels of land on Exmoor and then banning the Hunt from entering them. By 1985 the League owned about 1,200 acres in twenty-three properties out of a total Exmoor acreage of some 300,000. But, although the proportion of land owned by the League was tiny, its properties were carefully chosen to be on the run of the deer, and became a real thorn in the side of the Hunt. During the 1970s solicitors on behalf of the League wrote to the Masters complaining on a number of occasions of trespass by hounds on some of the League properties. In all cases the Master wrote apologising, undertaking that they would use their best endeavours to prevent further entries, and paying small sums by way of damages and costs.

Eventually the League issued a writ in the High Court alleging trespass on five properties including Pitleigh, near Wheddon Cross, and claiming a permanent injunction restraining the Hunt from entering any of the properties and from causing or permitting hounds to do so. The case was heard at Bristol before Mr Justice Park, and there were several days of evidence. Judgement was given on 2 April 1985. It was accepted that in no case had any damage been caused by the hounds, and the judge awarded a nominal sum of £25 damages for the entries by the hounds, but refused to order injunctions except in respect of Pitleigh. The judge found that there was evidence of persistent trespass by hounds on three occasions there, and ordered an injunction against the Masters restraining them or their mounted followers from causing or permitting hounds to enter the property. He also ordered the Hunt to pay the costs of the action, which amounted to £70,000.

By that time I had recently retired from the Court of Appeal, and was asked by the Committee to organise an appeal for the money. I approached the magazine *Horse and Hound,* and also the Masters of Foxhounds Association, the Chairman of which was Ronnie Wallace, Master of the Exmoor Foxhounds. Both were helpful and gave me their full support. *Horse and Hound* published a fund-raising letter from me supported by an Editorial, and the MFHA circulated all its members asking for contributions. Fortunately we were able to show that from the legal point of view the case had been a victory. The League had argued that a mere entry by hounds on land where no permission was given by the landowner constituted a trespass, regardless of the intention of the organiser of the hunt. The judge rejected that, holding that before a Master of Hounds may be held liable for trespass on land by hounds it had to be shown that he had been notified that hounds should not enter and that he either intended that the hounds should enter the land, or by negligence failed to prevent them from doing so. So we were able to put it to the hunting community that the outcome of the case was to the great benefit of hunting generally, and that the D&SS ought not to be left to pay the whole of the costs of that. The result was that the money flowed in, and in a remarkably short space of time we had the £70,000, and indeed more. Many individuals subscribed, and most Hunts organised a fund-raising event in support of the D&SS appeal.

The sequel to the case locally was that a deer fence was erected all round Pitleigh on land owned by other landowners, so that neither deer nor hounds could enter. I organised this venture. The cost of the materials was provided by the Hunt and the labour was given voluntarily by the members of the Hunt Supporters Club led by Peter Cox. It was carried out remarkably quickly and was a wonderful effort by the Hunt supporters. So hunting continued round Pitleigh.

CHAPTER V

The Scott Years
1987-2007

MAURICE SCOTT was born and brought up at Brendon Hill
Farm where his family farmed about 1,000 acres. I remember him as a boy winning most of the gymkhanas, where
he was almost unbeatable on his two ponies, Fairy and Cisco. He had
been a staghunter all his life, harbourer from 1976 to 1981 and Joint
Master with Norah Harding and Mike Robinson since 1981. In that
year, on their resignation, his wife Diana joined him in the mastership, thus beginning the longest mastership of the D&SS on record.
Diana was herself brought up on Exmoor, her father being "Bruin"
Milner-Brown, agent for the Molland and Hawkridge Estates and a
keen staghunter. After her marriage, Diana became a successful
breeder of event horses. Her foundation stallion was Ben Faerie, sire
of Priceless and Nightcap, both winners at Badminton.

Judy had never wanted me to be a judge, since her father had spent
half his working life on Circuit, and her mother had not enjoyed that
way of life. But when I was offered an appointment in 1968 she said,
"Of course you must take it. You are exhausted at the Bar. But I want
you to promise me that when you have done your fifteen years and
earned your index-linked pension you will retire to Lynch so we can
end our days hunting on Exmoor." So I retired in 1984 at the age of
67, which was considered young for a Lord Justice. I could have gone
on until I was 75. By that time we had sold Lynch with its stables,
and our horses were at livery with Tracey Andrews at Woodcocks Ley
Farm near Porlock, although she moved to Buckethole Farm the

following year. Sadly in 1985 Judy had a hip replacement which was unsuccessful, leaving her with no grip in one leg. She continued to ride and occasionally to hunt, but had two falls, the second in 1989 breaking two ribs. We decided it was too dangerous for her to continue hunting, so thereafter I hunted on my own, and occasionally with Allan's wife Loppy, until I gave up at the age of 80 in 1998.

It was the first time in my life that I was able to hunt regularly, and when Judy gave up I had two horses to ride, both greys, Spider and Fly. Both were good hunters, especially Fly, who had been placed in the Melton Cross Country race when owned by John George, father of Tom George the trainer. As well as hunting with the Exmoor and the Minehead Harriers, I hunted 33 days with the D&SS during the season 1985/86, 35 days 1986/87, 38 days 1987/88, 47 days 1988/89 and 35 days 1989/90. In that year I recorded in my hunting diary, "An Early Day Motion in Parliament to ban staghunting attracted over 200 signatures, but we are fighting back. Staghunting more popular than ever with 250 riders out in the Spring at Brendon Two Gates." In 1990/91 I had 41 days with the D&SS and the following year, 1991/92, 37 days. In that year Donald Summersgill, aged 23, the first whipper-in, took over from Dennis Boyles. I wrote in my hunting diary. "Donald made a brilliant start as huntsman killing a record number of hinds before Christmas. He has very good control of the hounds, and two very sharp young whippers-in, especially Martin, the 1st whipper-in. They all work as a team." In March of that year a Private Member's Bill in the House of Commons to ban all hunting was defeated by 12 votes. The Conservatives won the General Election by a narrow margin, which took the pressure off hunting. This season Mary Lycett-Green had joined the Scotts in the mastership. In 1992/93 I had 37 days with the D&SS, and in 1993/94 35. By this time I was beginning to funk very wet days in the winter, and in 1994/95 had only 22 days with the D&SS. This was largely because the Masters were suspended and all hunting stopped for five weeks following an incident in the Barle Valley in October, when a stag was shot four times in the neck before dying. It had a particularly strong ruff which old stags develop during the rut. The incident was videoed by

Donald Summersgill, Maurice Scott, Diana Scott and Mary Lycett Green

the League, a copy being sent to every MP, and caused an outcry in the press. Unfortunately both Dick Lloyd and Tom Yandle, who were Chairman and Vice Chairman of the Hunt Committee and of the Masters of Deerhounds Association, were abroad at the time; the matter was taken over by the British Field Sports Society, who set up a tribunal, ostensibly under the auspices of the Masters of Deerhounds Association, to investigate the matter under the Chairmanship of Lord Mancroft. The BFSS took the view that, if they had not taken charge, a bad situation would have become very much worse. But their intervention caused much anger on Exmoor since it is well known that at that time of year big stags are sometimes difficult to kill, and it was only a matter of seconds before this stag was killed. It was some considerable time before relations between the BFSS and the D&SS were restored.

Sadly Judy died of bronchial pneumonia in 1995. Once again I had only 22 days staghunting. I had 29 days in 1996/97, by which time I had had to say goodbye to my two old greys. I replaced them with a very good little mare called Gambol, which I bought from Kevin Lamacraft who runs the Equitation Centre at Knowle, near Timberscombe. She was well bred, fast and sure footed, but sensible and manageable by a 79-year-old. Tracey Andrews had decided to give up taking liveries, so I sent Gambol to Jeanette Branton at the White Horse Yard at Exford, from where I had a very good last season. I had remarried in 1997, to Joan Dennehy, and although she urged me to go on hunting I decided to give up when I was 80. I still enjoyed the actual hunting, except in the winter, which I gave up during the last season, but was finding the whole business of driving the horse to the meet, parking, unboxing, mounting, then boxing the horse at the end of the day, increasingly wearisome. Unfortunately my daughter-in-law Loppy preferred jump-hunting and kept a horse with the Blackmore Vale and then with the Taunton Vale. So I was on my own. My last day was 28 April 1998, when we had a ringing hunt on the Forest from Wellshead and the Masters kindly gave me a stag's head.

During those years I had some very good days hunting. Most of these were on the North Forest, where it is open and the going good, but the deer tended to run in circles, so there was seldom a good point. An exception was 2 September 1986, when a stag found at Tenerdy from a meet at Blackmore Gate ran over the Chains to Dry Bridges on the Brendon Road, where the pack was laid on. They ran over Brendon Common, Badgworthy, Deer Park, Alderman's Barrow, Dunkery, and down Bincombe to the Cutcombe Covers, where they killed. This was a 12-mile point almost straight over the moor.

Another good hunt was from Exford on 6 October 1987. They found on Staddon Hill and ran to Pennycombe, where the pack was laid on; then by Picked Stones, up the Barle by Cow Castle to Blue Gate, across Boundary Road at Comerslade, over Whitefield Down to East Down Wood, and through Hole where, following an hour's hunting in the wood, during which the stag stood to bay three times and broke away, he was killed at 4.25pm, the pack having been laid on at 1.30pm. I wrote in my diary, "This was the best hunt I have had for many years. Not fast because the scent was patchy and the stag never waited. It seemed like a Bray stag but the experts said it was an Exe stag that knew his way. It was a 12 mile point from Staddon Hill to Newtown Bridge but about 17 as hounds ran."

We had a marvellous hind hunt on my 70th birthday, 16 January 1988, from a meet at Alderman's Barrow. A single hind was found in the Exe near Riscombe, which turned up below Warren Farm and out over Pinford and Buscombe to Badgworthy Plantation; then over the Deer Park and Mill Hill to Weir Wood and back to Acmead, and down Weir Water to Robbers Bridge, where they killed at 1.45pm. This was a typical day's hind hunting on the Forest, all at top speed on a glorious sunny day. I was given a slot as a birthday present.

There were two very good days spring staghunting in 1990, the first from Blackmore Gate on 24 March. Once again found in Tenerdy, the pack laid on at Scob Hill Gate at 1.25pm. Ran over Tippacott Ridge to the Badgworthy and up Clannacombe to South Common, Chalk Water Weir Water and killed at 3.15pm below Lucott Cross. An 11-mile point. On 31 March from Sandyway we found low down in Long Wood and ran up nearly to the boundary road before turning back to Barcombe Down, where the pack was

Dennis Boyles, with hounds, moving off from a meet at Porlock Weir, followed by Donald Summersgill, Martin Watts and Diana Scott

laid on at 1.15pm. They ran straight down to South Wood and into hinds. After much stopping of hounds on false scents, the stag ran up to Barcombe Down at 2.30pm and crossed the North Molton Ridge to Sandyway Cross, where they checked. Hit off the line by the Sportsman's Arms pub and ran by Litton and Willingford to Lords. Turned sharp across the Hawkridge road past Cloggs to Lyshwell, where there were more hinds. After sorting these out they ran over Anstey Common, past Anstey Barrows and Guphill, skirted West Anstey church and ran almost to the A361. Turned back and killed at Yeo Mill at 5.15pm. A 13-mile furthest point. My horse lost a shoe so I pulled up at Shircombe when the hounds were in Lyshwell.

20 April 1991 was an outstanding day for the D&SS. It was Dennis Boyles' last day after twenty years as huntsman, and there were about 300 people mounted at the kennels, including eleven Hunt servants all wearing livery. There were also hundreds of cars and foot followers. £22,000 was raised for Dennis's testimonial, and

Dick Lloyd, Chairman, presenting Dennis Boyles with his testimonial,
20 April 1991

it was arranged he would live at Honeymead. The tufters were taken
straight to the Forest, and laid on to a herd of about fifty deer on
Lannacombe Plain. Fortunately a one-horned stag left the herd and
ran over the Exe to the Windbreak, where it was fresh found, and ran
back over Warren Plain and down Buscombe to Toms Hill, when the
pack was laid on at 1.30pm. They ran well over Kittucks and Mill Hill
to Weir Water, where the stag turned back by the beach fence. They

fresh found in Weir Water and ran up to Alderman's Barrow; turned over Hurdle Down and killed in Embercombe at 3pm. Although there was no great point and the scent was patchy it was a marvellous clear, sunny day when everything went right.

On 28 September 1991 there was a Memorial Meet for Sir Bernard Waley-Cohen at Honeymead. There were 1,000 people at the Meet, including nearly 300 mounted, in spite of heavy rain. We spent the morning on the Forest and the afternoon round Honeymead.

On 12 October we met at Alderman's Barrow, when a fine stag and two hinds were found in Exe Cleeve and ran across Hayes Allotment to Swap Hill, where the pack was laid on, and ran back to the Exe, where the deer divided and the hounds were put on to the stag. They ran up over Red Stone, crossed the road by Red Deer and ran past Picked Stones to the Barle. Ran up the water past Simonsbath and Cornham to Aclands, turned up past Moles Chamber and Five Cross Ways, and killed in the Bray. A 10-mile point. I wrote in my diary, "A proper hunt but unusual line."

This was the beginning of a very good fortnight, when I hunted on four days: Tuesday 15th at Hawkridge, Thursday 17th at Pitcombe Head, Monday 21st at the Porlock Parks and Tuesday 22nd at Dunkery Hill Gate. On each day we had a hunt, the best being from the Porlock Parks, when they found in Greencombe and ran out to Whit Stones, where the pack was laid on. They ran through the Shillets and Bromham gutters to Acmead and Larkbarrow, then over Badgworthy crossing the Brendon Road at Scob Hill Gate over Twitchen Ridge and back over Pinford to Wellshead, where they killed. A great hunt.

On 11 December 1991 we met at Hawkcombe Head and had two very good hind hunts on the Forest. I wrote in my diary, "Two very good hunts ruined by John Lytton's ban on hounds entering Lillycombe." A commercial pheasant shoot had just been started there. On 11 March 1992 we met at Cuzzicombe Post. I had two of my Clifford granddaughters with me and a friend of theirs, all mounted. We laid on to four stags in Gatcombe, but one turned back to Cuzzicombe and White Post, where the pack was laid on. We then ran fast over Soggy Moor, where I led the girls into a large hole – but all survived. We ran on over Molland Moor to Lyshwell and the Danesbrook, where we killed above Slade Bridge. They laid on again at Venford and ran over East Anstey Common and down to Beer, when we went home after a good gallop on the moor.

On 12 September 1992 the meet was at Brendon Two Gates. We found a big stag, obviously not from the Forest, in the Exe below Prayway Head, which after a loop round Pinford ran up to Warren Gate, where the pack was laid on at 12.30pm. They ran over Honeymead and the Barle, up Kinsford Water to the Boundary Road. We crossed Fyldon Common and ran down Lyddicombe to Heasley Mill and on to the Bray, where they checked. Hit off the line by Rabscott and ran by Charles Bottom and East Buckland over Huxtable, past Buckinghams and Illers Leary to Riverton, where they killed at 4.15pm, all his rights and four on both sides. A 12-mile point. Hounds hunted well as the scent was not good and the stag kept moving. I finished drinking whisky with Lady Margaret Fortescue at Castle Hill and was taken back to Honeymead with the Lloyds, where I was picked up by Robert Andrews. Home at 7.15pm. Not bad for a 75-year-old. We had had another good day from Nutscale Drive on 8 August when three stags had been killed, which I believe to be a record.

The 1996 spring staghunting was as good as I ever remember, when we had some outstanding hunts. Loppy and I went to Honeymead Cross on 23 March. A single stag ran down Exe Cleeve to Riscombe Down, to Muddicombe. We crossed the Simonsbath road at Thorne to Lyncombe, where the pack was laid on at 1.30pm. Crossed Staddon Hill with the stag 40 minutes ahead. We ran over Kemps, across the Exe to Bye Hill, across Ash Lane to Burrow Wood and over Halse Lane to Yellowcombe, where the stag laid up. After extensive casting he was fresh found and killed at 3.30pm. Although this was not a good riding hunt, as we were mostly on roads and tracks, it was a 10-mile point over a very unusual line.

On 20 April Loppy and I went to Exford, where there was a presentation for Dick Lloyd on his retirement as Chairman of the Hunt

Philip Hawkins, Jack Dallyn, Dennis Boyles and Maurice Scott

Committee. With a mounted field of 300, we laid on to a bunch of deer in Ramscombe. A single deer came up Orchard Bottom to Hayes Allotment, where the pack was laid on at 12.15pm. They ran over Pinford and Buscombe to Lannacombe, and Hoccombe to Withycombe ridge, over Lankcombe to the Badgworthy. The stag then retraced his steps back over Brendon Common to Warren; then back a second time to Badgworthy, and out again to kill in Hoccombe Water at 5.30pm. Some stag! An exceptionally hard day for horses. Hounds ran for 35 miles without crossing a road. Loppy and I were not at the kill. Very few were. I rode Spider, our combined ages being 100.

On 25 April we met at Webbers Post. We found a single stag in Mansley Combe, which ran straight over Dunkery to Chetsford, where he joined a herd. Hounds hunted on by Lucott Cross, Colley Water, Black Barrow, Mill Hill and Deer Park to Warren. Then back to Badgworthy, where they lost after another good galloping day on the Forest.

During 1996 we had a very good September, including the Barnstaple Fair meet at Yarde Down on the 21st, to which Loppy and I went. Seven stags came out of Halscombe in all directions. Two ran

Donald Summersgill and Martin walking hounds out at Exford. The huntsman, two whippers-in and the kennelman work in the kennels, ensuring that the hounds are kept fit for their nine-month season three days a week in all weathers.

over Great Woolcombe to the Barle below Picked Stones and down to Sherdon Hutch, where they divided. One ran down the water, the other up. Hounds ran up to Halscombe Plantation where another stag joined in. The hunted stag crossed the road and ran on by Cornham Ford, Roostitchen and Challacombe. They killed in the Bray below Wallover. The hind hunting was as good as I remember, with a good hunt every day and sometimes two at the same time. By this time Philip Hawkins of Warren Farm had joined the mastership and the tufters were divided, with Donald and Maurice Scott taking one lot and the first whipper-in, Martin Watts, and Philip the other. This was done in order to maximise the cull of hinds. Spring staghunting in March was also first class, but April was disappointing due to dry weather and poor scent.

1997/98 was my last season. Sadly Philip Hawkins had a heart attack and died at a meet early in the season. We had some good days in the autumn, including a 9-mile point from Brendon Two Gates on 23 September. We found in Tangs Combe at 12pm, crossing the Challacombe road at Cornham and turning over Ricksy Ball by Smallacombe, Vintcombe, Moles Chamber, Shoulsbarrow, Wallover Down to Leworthy Bridge. We killed on Bratton Down at 2.30pm. The spring staghunting was disappointing; the weather was awful and I came back soaked several times. My last day was on 28 April at Wellshead. We laid on to the largest herd I ever saw, about 100 hinds with three spring stags, which by a miracle eventually left the herd and ran into Exe Cleeve with two hinds. The tufters ran up Orchard Combe by Larkbarrow to Chalk Water, down to Robbers Bridge, then up Weir Water almost to Lucott Cross. When they turned out over Acmead towards Hayes Allotment I decided to go home, the weather was so stormy.

I hope these accounts of hunts with the D&SS will give an idea even to people unfamiliar with Exmoor of what it was like when it was allowed to be done properly. The length of the hunts and the skill required to keep hounds on the hunted deer were unique to staghunting. The Hunt servants worked as a team, and there were several knowledgeable farmers who helped. It was an immensely

Three second horsemen, David Grills, Raymond Dart and Barry Tiller.
Always immaculately turned out, the second horse "persons",
(they are often girls), are much admired and never fail to
produce the pack at the right place and the right time.

popular sport, like Premier Football in an industrial town, and followed by people of all ages and classes. It was also the most effective
and humane way of managing the deer and minimising the damage
they cause farmers, while at the same time maintaining a healthy herd
which is such a feature of Exmoor.

The social and economic benefits of staghunting are well known
and well documented. In 1991 the Centre for Rural Studies at
the Royal Agricultural College, Cirencester, was commissioned by the
National Trust to report on the "Economic and Social Aspects of Deer
Hunting on Exmoor and the Quantocks". It reported in 1993. The
report listed the large numbers of social activities linked to the Hunts
in what is an exceptionally remote area compared with other parts
of the United Kingdom. Most Exmoor hill farmers and their families
live isolated and lonely lives, and for many their sole recreation

Hope Bourne on foot at a meet at Molland Moor Gate.
She lived for 25 years in a caravan on the moor, near Withypool,
and has written charming books about her life on the moor,
which she loves.

revolves round the Hunt and its activities. Moreover large numbers of pensioners and others regularly follow the hunts in motor cars, enjoying a picnic in beautiful surroundings, with the interest of the hunt and the companionship of their peers. The Centre for Rural Studies' report noted that during the season 1990/91 the subscribers of the D&SS spent about £3.5 million on their hunting, virtually all in local purchases from feed merchants, blacksmiths, saddlers, outfitters, garages and others. This figure, which has no doubt increased over the years, does not include the expenditure of visitors, of whom there are a large number, who either ride or follow the hounds in motor cars. Staghunting on Exmoor is a unique experience. Many come to Exmoor for a holiday to follow the hounds, and stay in local hotels or bed and breakfast accommodation. All this adds to the economic benefits of staghunting, which certainly before the Hunting Act 2004 made a significant contribution to the fragile economies of North Devon and West Somerset.

CHAPTER VI

The Badgworthy Land Company

IN 1926 Sir Brian Mountain, Chairman of the Eagle Star Insurance Company, put the Oare Manor Estate on the market. This included the Deer Park, part of the Badgworthy valley, and Brendon Common, all prime staghunting country. The D&SS Hunt Committee decided that it should be bought on behalf of the Hunt, and the cost (£7,750) was raised from the subscribers. It was then decided that the property should be vested in a company, independent of the Hunt, and so the Badgworthy Land Company, whose shares were limited by guarantee, was formed. In 1957 Mr Slater of Woolhanger died, leaving moorland to the west of the Brendon road, including Ilkerton Ridge, to the Company. This raised its holding to about 7,000 acres of moorland in the heart of Exmoor. The Hunt also transferred the kennels at Exford to the Company.

The Company was run by a board consisting of ten directors, with Lord Poltimore as Chairman. The Secretary was Smyth-Richards, the agent of the Castle Hill estate, who had an unrivalled knowledge of the moor. Since virtually the whole of the Company's land was moorland which was let to hill farmers on grazing leases, very little management was required, and the directors' meetings were informal affairs. After the Second World War Colonel Guy Jackson, DSO, the Master of the Exmoor Foxhounds, was the Chairman and my father-in-law Toby Pilcher one of the directors. The AGM was held on Exford Show day behind the stand on the old showground.

By this time the League Against Cruel Sports was beginning to buy land on Exmoor, and this coincided with the death of Maurice

Houlder, who had been Joint Master of the D&SS from 1945 to 1948. He was Chairman of Houlder Brothers, a shipping line, and had a house at Twitchen in the Exe Valley. He also owned three farms, Ford, Walland and North Hill, which were great strongholds for the deer since they included Blagdon Wood. When Houlder died the farms were put up for sale. My father-in-law went to see "Crow" Smith-Bingham, who was a rich retired stockbroker living at Melcombe at Exford, and a keen staghunter. He persuaded "Crow" to buy the farms and give them to the Badgworthy Land Company. The acreage was not large but of great importance from the point of view of the deer.

At about this time the owner of Baronsdown near Dulverton was in financial difficulties and threatening to sell to the League. Auberon Herbert of Pixton Park lent him a substantial sum of money secured by a mortgage on the property, which contained a clause that nothing should be done to prevent hunting at Baronsdown. The League redeemed the mortgage, which could not be prevented under the law. They then granted another mortgage containing a restriction on all hunting, and finally acquired the property, banning the Hunt from it, and naming it as a deer "sanctuary". This was a serious matter since Baronsdown is in the Exe Valley and a stronghold for the deer.

The Badgworthy Land Company realised that it would have to be more active in acquiring land to protect hunting. But although it had substantial land holdings it had virtually no cash. Guy Jackson suggested that the Company should acquire sporting rights, i.e. shooting and fishing rights. But these were expensive and becoming increasingly valuable.

My father-in-law then consulted John Pennycuick, a leading Chancery QC who became Vice Chancellor. He advised that a "hunting right" was a right known to the law and that it "ran with the land". That is to say it was binding not only as between the original grantor and grantee but also on all subsequent owners of the land. The right simply prevented the landowner from taking action for trespass if the hunt crossed the land. It was granted to the Badgworthy Land Company which licensed the local Hunts, including the D&SS, to exercise it. The right has never been challenged in the Courts, and indeed has been used by the League.

A campaign was then started by the Company to acquire hunting rights. The first donors were the Fortescue Estate, who at that time owned large areas of the moor, including the Challacombe Estate and Simonsbath. Since that land was owned by trustees, it was necessary for a payment to be made for the hunting rights. But that is the only occasion on which payment has been made for hunting rights, the Company maintaining that they have no market value. Since then the Company has acquired hunting rights over a very large area of Exmoor, about 60,000 acres. These have come in all sizes, some covering large areas but mostly small parcels of land of less than 100 acres. In some cases hunting rights have been bequeathed by will. The right appears on the deeds of the property so is available to a purchaser during a pre-purchase search of the documents. The fact that hunting rights have been given over such a large area shows the support for hunting which exists among landowners on the moor.

Each director of the Company owned a qualifying share, the balance being owned by the Chairman. In the seventies Capital Transfer Tax, the predecessor of Capital Gains Tax, was introduced. This meant that on each change of a director CTT would be payable on his share, which in the case of the Chairman would amount to a substantial sum. It was therefore decided in 1982 that a charity would be formed and that all the shares in the Company would be owned by the charity, which would be exempt from CTT. The charity was duly set up following negotiations between Bernard Waley-Cohen, Chairman at the time, myself and the Chairman of the Charities Commission. The charity was called the Badgworthy Trust for the Preservation of Exmoor, its objects being the preservation of Exmoor and its heritage including the encouragement of recreation. All shares in the Company were transferred to the Trust, and three of the directors were appointed trustees.

These arrangements naturally affected the policy of the Company. Instead of being an adjunct of the Hunt it was effectively a charity, bound to follow its charitable objects. This involved a balance between conservation on the one side and hunting on the other. The directors took the view that there was no serious dichotomy between them, since the welfare of the herd of wild red deer, one of the historic features of Exmoor, was best achieved through the traditional management of the Hunt. And of course the majority of the Company's property had been acquired by the Hunt subscribers, and given to the Company.

The Company is well-placed to assist in the objects of the Charitable Trust, owning some 7,300 acres (2,954 hectares); in addition the Trust owns some 73 acres of woodland in its own right. The majority of the Company's land ownership comprises open moorland, but also includes some 555 acres (225 hectares) of woodland and two traditional hill farms.

Within the Company's ownership are such well-known sites as the Doone Country of Badgworthy, Snowdrop Valley at Cutombe, and Brendon and Lynton Commons. The whole of the Company's land is designated as an Environmentally Sensitive Area (ESA) and most lies within Sites of Special Scientific Interest and designated SAC. The Company is fortunate to own important habitats such as blanket bog, upland heath and upland oak woods – areas that are home to endangered species of national importance, including butterflies, (the heath and high brown fritillaries), merlins, and lichens; and species with an uncertain future such as the red deer. The Company is active in the promotion of conservation measures, working closely with English Nature (EN). Works have included the limitation of the spread of rhododendron ponticum on open moor-land, the creation and preservation of habitat, and steps to enhance the management of specific areas, as well as supporting the welfare and proper management of particular species. The Company believes that it is the proper conservation of Exmoor that will ensure its protection and benefit the public. This includes the conservation and interpretation of the historic landscape, and the Company has been involved with the Exmoor National Park Authority (ENPA) in recording and preparing action plans for protecting archaeological sites, and providing interpretation for visitors such as the Badg-worthy leaflet and signboards at Snowdrop Valley.

The Company entered all its in-hand land into the Exmoor Environmentally Sensitive Area management schemes and encouraged its tenants to do so. It has also actively assisted the graziers on its Commons to enter agri-environmental management agreements. The Company is now converting all its ESA agreements into the Environmental Stewardship Scheme (Higher Level Scheme), the Company's aim being to conserve the moorland through managed grazing and positive conservation management, while ensuring that the commoners are compensated for any limitations on their rights for the period of the agreement. The Company is pursuing better management of its woodland (through woodland certification) and, where the principle concern is ecological rather than silvicultural, this management includes improved public access. The Company is carrying out a major restoration scheme at Sherracombe involving replacing conifer plantations with oak and heath.

The Company has always supported public access. Brendon Common was dedicated as access land under Section 193 of the Law of Property Act 1925, which allows individuals to enjoy the area on foot and on horseback (subject to bylaws). The Company encourages recreation on foot to its areas of moorland and upon public bridleways and footpaths through woodland. The Company recognises that access management is necessary in order to balance all the requirements and interests concerning its land and works closely with the ENPA and its Rangers to ensure that, as far as is possible all needs are met. Recently this has included the creation of new permissive bridleways and the upgrading of footpaths, including works for improving access for people with disabilities.

The Company supports all appropriate forms of leisure activity that are compatible with preserving Exmoor. This does mean, in certain circumstances, that public access should be temporarily or permanently excluded or discouraged. Guidance is taken from appropriate bodies and the considerable local knowledge available to the Company. In addition, assessment of risk indicates that public access to all Company property is inadvisable because of natural or man-made hazards and that certain properties, particularly working farms, houses and businesses are inappropriate for access other than on definitive rights of way. This means that historically the Company has not encouraged public access to its entire landholding.

The Company supports events across its land such as the Golden Horseshoe (endurance riding), mountain biking, orienteering, walking for charitable purposes, and arduous training and other events and outdoor activities including, of course, hunting.

The Company believes that such organised leisure activities and events should be carried out in a safe manner, and at times which do not conflict with nature (the bird nesting season etc) or damage the environment or conflict with other activities. To achieve this, the Company licences establishments such as pony trekking centres and advocates the ENPA protocol for organised events. In assisting events organisers, the Company co-operates with the ENPA, EN and other bodies to avoid conflicts between conservation and recreation. We have had to join with the ENPA, the police and other bodies in discouraging damaging activities and those contrary to bylaws and the Company require indemnity insurance from commercial users and the holders of events.

Future benefits are ensured by considering public benefit in planning management tasks and projects; for example with the England Woodland Grant Scheme and within the Sherracombe Project to restore conifer woodland to upland oak wood. This project will include public access and interpretation (including the Sherracombe Roman iron-smelting activity).

The Company is actively involved in the consultation stages of various pieces of Government legislation that could or does affect Exmoor and the Trust's charitable objectives.

In 1986 Bernard Waley-Cohen retired, on account of ill health, and I became Chairman, having been a director for some years. My first concern was to increase the liquidity of the Company. The farmhouse at Walland had been used as a cow barn and hay store since the 1920s and was effectively derelict. My plan was to obtain planning permission for it to be converted into a dwelling-house, and then sell it on the open market. It was in a superb position, facing south, overlooking the Avill Valley, with a mild climate. But the planning committee of the Exmoor National Park turned down our application. So we appealed to an Inspector, before whom I appeared myself, and managed to persuade him that our plan was acceptable. We built a modern cow barn for our tenant, Edgar Webber, and put the farmhouse up for auction. It made £86,000, a substantial sum in those days, and was bought by a developer who converted it into a beautiful house, now occupied by a retired ambassador whose wife hunts. This gave the Company a sum of cash which enabled us to make some modest purchases and improved our financial position generally.

At that time the Secretary of the Company was Robert Humphreys, who was married to one of Diana Scott's sisters. He had succeeded his father-in-law, "Bruin" Milner-Brown, as agent to the Molland Estate. But after a few years he retired, to settle in the West Indies, and was succeeded by Jeremy Holtam, a land agent practising in Barnstaple. Jeremy was a conservationist and very skilled in obtaining grants for various projects from the National Park, Government and the European Union. These enabled us to carry out much needed forestry work in the Company's woodlands and generally to improve the estate. The present Secretary is Hugh Thomas, formerly agent to the Castle Hill estate.

I retired as Chairman in 2000 and was succeeded by Sir Hugh Stucley, grandson of Lord Poltimore, the first Chairman, and a large and experienced landowner in North Devon. He retired in 2005 and was succeeded by Tom Yandle, now also Chairman of the D&SS Committee.

The Badgworthy Land Company is often seen as the vehicle for the acquisition of hunting rights. But it is much more than that. After the National Trust, it is the largest private landowner on Exmoor and is an important conservation body with, because of its history, a special interest in the deer.

CHAPTER VII

The National Trust

T HE NATIONAL TRUST is the largest private landowner on Exmoor, owning about 12,000 acres; 3,000 of those, the Dunkery Estate, were donated in 1935 by Colonel Wiggin, Master of the D&SS, and my first wife's grandmother, Mrs Allan Hughes. The deed of gift contained a covenant that the Trust "will not at any time prevent the said land being used for the purpose of the hunting of deer, foxes or hares". The Trust also granted the donors a 99-year lease of the sporting rights over Dunkery.

In 1944 Sir Richard Acland gave the adjoining Holnicote Estate of about 10,000 acres to the Trust. He also gave another estate, Killerton, near Exeter, at the same time. On 1 April 1943 the Secretary of the National Trust wrote to the Trust's solicitors, saying, "The deed to provide also that staghunting is to be permitted to take place on the Holnicote Estate as long as it is permitted to take place on a substantial majority of the adjoining lands." At about the same time Sir Richard wrote, concerning the Deed of Gift, "Preservation of staghunting and foxhunting while permitted on the substantial part of adjoining property to be included in the deed of transfer." In his memorandum of wishes of 10 January 1944, Sir Richard wrote, "In transferring my Killerton and Holnicote Estates to the National Trust I am confident that they will respect my wishes though I recognise that they are under no legal obligation to do so … I have already arranged that staghunting and foxhunting is to be permitted on the Holnicote Estate so long as the sport is carried on over a substantial part of the adjoining lands and I hope that every effort will be made for the opening meet of the Stag Hounds to be held at Cloutsham as heretofore."

Despite the clear instructions both by the Secretary of the Trust and Sir Richard himself, there was no mention of hunting in the Deed of Gift. There was no question of Sir Richard having changed his mind. In an interview on BBC radio on 6 November 1990, following the passing of an anti-staghunting resolution at the AGM of the National Trust, Sir Richard said, "I would regard it as a great betrayal if they attached more importance to this tiny minority than the expressed wishes of the donor, and through the whole of the coming century I would think that such an action on behalf of the Council would enormously diminish the amount of property which would be offered to the Trust." These views were also published in an article in *The Field* in December 1990 and a letter to the *Times* on 6 November, shortly before Sir Richard died. The most likely explanation is that inclusion of the hunting provision was simply overlooked in the very large number of items which had to be included in the Deed for both properties.

Following the Second World War the Trust's policy with regard to hunting on its land was that, where it had been traditional, it should be allowed to continue. The Trust also had a policy that wherever possible the wishes of donors of property should always be followed, whether legally binding or not. The first Trust agent at Holnicote was Colonel Freddy Reeks, who before the war had been agent of both the Holnicote and Killerton estates on behalf of the Acland family. He was a keen supporter of hunting. In the 1970s Major Guy Courage, DSO was appointed agent at Holnicote. He also was a supporter of hunting and indeed died of a heart attack while riding to hounds. I became Chairman of the local advisory Committee of the National Trust in 1963, and remained until 1981, when Regional Committees were established and local committees abolished. During all that period relations between the Trust and the Hunt were extremely cordial, and the Trust fully accepted and supported the traditional method of deer management through the Hunt.

In about 1988 the League encouraged its members to join the Trust and to oppose hunting on Trust property, although it stated publicly that it did not suggest that hunting should be banned in cases where the donor had clearly stated that it should continue. However, an AGM members' resolution was proposed in 1990 which sought to prohibit deer hunting on the Trust's property. This was carried by some 69,000 votes to 68,000, a tiny minority bearing in mind that the Trust's membership at that time was approaching two million. Moreover the comparatively small number of voters demonstrated that the issue of hunting was a low priority with most members.

The response of the Council was twofold. Firstly, they invited a retired Law Lord, Lord Oliver, who had been a contemporary of mine in the Court of Appeal, to report on the Constitution of the Trust, which is contained in an Act of Parliament. He held that the Trust was not a democratic institution but was a public charity managed by its Council. He said, "The Council does not exist to serve the membership but to administer a public charity so as best to effect the purposes for which it was established."

The Council also set up a Working Party under the chairmanship of Professor Savage to consider the conservation, deer management, legal, economic and social implications of a ban on deer hunting on Trust property. The Working Party concluded that the Trust should continue to allow deer hunting to continue on its property, concluding, "to continue the necessary active co-operation from landowners and farmers which is essential to the welfare of the deer, the role of the Hunt is of critical importance."

On 16 July 1994, at an Extraordinary General Meeting of the Trust, a resolution was carried by some 115,000 to 100,000 votes that the Trust should set up a working party to address the issues of cruelty and animal welfare in deer hunting, which had not been within the terms of reference of the Savage Enquiry. On 19 July I wrote to Sir Angus Stirling, Director General of the Trust, referring him to his letter to me of 3 November 1993, in which he had re-affirmed the Trust's policy on hunting and confirmed that the Council was determined to respect the wishes of donors, and that there was no question of changing the status quo at Holnicote or Dunkery. I added, "The consequence of that policy is that the Trust could not ban hunting on its Exmoor Estate whatever the result of any ballot or recommendations of any working party. Ever since the first anti-hunting vote at the AGM I have pressed first the Chairman [Lord Chorley] and then yourself to take the stand that the hands of the Trust are tied with regard to hunting on Exmoor, and that working parties and ballots are a waste of time and money." I also drew attention to the Oliver report, pointing out that the effects of hunting had nothing to do with the purposes for which the Trust was established, which were basically the preservation of its properties for the benefit of the public. Sir Angus replied on 4 August, saying at the outset, "I will confirm again in case there is any doubt that the Trust has no intention of altering the status quo by banning hunting (so long as it is a legal activity) on its Exmoor properties, where the donor's wishes clearly stipulated that field sports should continue." But he went on to say that the vote at the EGM had made the position of the Council more difficult, and that there was a risk that, if they ignored the majority vote altogether, they might be faced with a vote of no confidence in the Council.

In the result the Council appointed Professor Bateson to study the effect of hunting with hounds on the welfare of deer. Professor Bateson was Provost of King's College, Cambridge, a Professor of Ethnology and a former director of the sub-department of Animal Behaviour at the University. He was accompanied by an assistant, Dr Elizabeth Bradshaw, and announced that they wished to take samples of the blood of deer killed by the Hunt. The Hunt gave them full co-operation and the samples were taken by the Hunt staff. In return Professor Bateson said that his report would be shown to the Hunt for its comments before being sent to the National Trust.

Professor Bateson invited a panel of thirteen experts on such subjects as deer management, veterinary science, physiology and animal behaviour to advise him in the production of his report. The panel met twice during the work, which was complete by the end of 1996. Instead of notifying the Hunt of his findings as agreed, Professor

Bateson held a private meeting at King's College on 13 January 1997. By that time there was a new Chairman of the National Trust, Charles Nunneley, and a new Director General, Martin Drury. In addition to them, the meeting was attended by the Deputy Chairman, Jonathan Peel, and Deputy Director Julian Prideaux. At the meeting Professor Bateson summarised the conclusions of his report. Following this the Chairman set up a group chaired by the Deputy Chairman to advise and make recommendations to him for presenting the report. The group took the view that "the evidence now presented by the Bateson Report is so compelling as to leave the Trust with no choice … but to override the obligation accepted under the terms of a donor's memorandum of wishes."

The Chairman arranged a press conference on 9 April at which he announced to the assembled press that he proposed to recommend to the Council that, as a result of the Bateson Report, licences should not be issued to permit deer hunting on Trust properties. On the same day copies of the 77-page report and a paper by the Chairman were delivered in the morning by hand to all members of the Council, who consequently had very little opportunity of considering or digesting the report. The Council met at a Special Meeting the following day, when Professor Bateson introduced his report and summarised his conclusions. He then left the room when there was a discussion and the Council agreed unanimously to end deer hunting with hounds on Trust land.

This decision provoked widespread criticism, not only from hunting people but also from members of the Trust who were shocked that Sir Richard Acland's wishes should have been ignored, and from scientists who were critical of the science and of the methodology used in compiling the report.

Professor Bateson's terms of reference were narrow. They were "To study suffering as a welfare factor in the management of red deer on National Trust properties on Exmoor and the Quantock Hills", having regard to certain criteria including "the likely effects so far as they can be estimated of a hunting ban on suffering among deer and to report". Bateson reached a clear conclusion, which he described as "the key conclusion", namely that "hunting with hounds can no longer be justified on welfare grounds", but he went on to say in the same paragraph, "I accept that the National Trust will want to weigh this conclusion against other issues, including their wider responsibilities, considerations about the social and economic benefits of hunting and the problems of conservation." The action of the Chairman in calling a press conference the day before the Council meeting, at which he announced that he proposed to recommend a ban on deer hunting, meant that the Council was put in an impossible position. Unless they jettisoned their Chairman, there could be no balancing of Bateson's "key" conclusion against other relevant factors mentioned by him. The Council was presented with a *fait accompli.*

The report itself could not be described as a scientific document. Its conclusions were stated in clear language easily understood by a layman. But none of the data on which they were based were published, so it was impossible for there to be a full scientific appraisal of the work. Much use was made of generalities. For example, the phrase "an unacceptable level of suffering" was repeated throughout the report but there was no indication of what was meant by it or how comparisons were made, or when acceptable suffering became unacceptable.

There was criticism from the scientific world of the fact that the report was never subjected to the normal process of peer review, which is invariably required before the recommendations of scientific papers are implemented. Bateson asserted that his self-appointed panel of experts was more effective than a peer review. But this was not accepted by other scientists, and a group of scientists and veterinarians was set up to attempt a similar exercise to check Bateson's conclusions.

This group was led by Professor Roger Harris of the Royal Veterinary College, London, and its report presented by Professor L.B. Jeffcott of the Department of Clinical Veterinary Medicine at Cambridge University was entitled "The physiological response of red deer to prolonged exercise undertaken during hunting". It was called "The

Joint Universities Study on Deer Hunting". The main thrust of the Bateson Report had been, not the circumstances of the actual kill, but of the chase itself. The report concluded that the suffering caused to the deer after a hunt was "unacceptable". Professor Harris's team took blood samples from hunted and stalked deer from January to May 1998 and reported in 1999. Its key conclusion was that the exercise taken by deer for all but the last minutes of a hunt was well within their physiological capacity (i.e. at a level not immediately leading to fatigue or exhaustion), and found that Professor Bateson's conclusion that pursuit by hounds pushed deer far beyond normal physiological limits were not supported by their findings.

Meanwhile the Hunt started legal proceedings with an application for Judicial Review of the decision of the Council of 10 April 1997. Application was made for an interim injunction restraining the Trust from enforcing its ban pending the hearing of this Review. The case came before Mr Justice Walker (now Lord Walker), who gave judgement on 21 August 1997. Although he declined to order an interim injunction on the ground that that would effectively be deciding the main application, the judge was critical of the way in which the decision had been made. He said, "The decision on 10 April last seems to me to have been rushed, to say the least. The procedure of holding a press conference the day before the meeting, however well intentioned, seems to me very questionable." Earlier he had said, "I do have the strong impression that the Chairman and Deputy Chairman's group were preoccupied with the need (especially for media purposes) to reach a quick clear decision. That seems to have led to secrecy being preferred to an opportunity for consultation or discussion as had been promised by Professor Bateson to the Master of Staghounds, and to a programme which must have put great pressure on even the most diligent and receptive Council members. Moreover I have to say that I see great force in the submission that, if calm private discussion was the object to be achieved, it was an extraordinary decision to present the Bateson Report at a press conference on the day before the meeting." Later the judge said, "I think that there is evidence of what seems to me to have been a serious error of judgement about the speed and secrecy with which the decision was taken. Controversial topics are bound to be controversial, and no amount of media management can avoid that. As it was, if Council members were intended to be able to reach their decision in a calm and cloistered way on 10 April 1997 the fact is that they were faced already in the newspapers on the morning of 10 April with a good deal of media comment on the Chairman's press conference." And the judge suggested that the Council should meet again to reconsider its decision in the light of the objections by the Hunt.

The Council duly met on 2 October 1997. Once again Professor Bateson and Dr Bradshaw were present as the Trust's scientific advisers. But although a detailed briefing paper had been prepared by the Chairmen of both the D&SS and Quantock Staghounds, neither of them was allowed to attend the meeting, although they had offered to do so. The briefing paper was dismissed by the Chairman as making "many points well worthy of attention but also included a large number of half truths, misrepresentations and unsupported allegations". After the Chairman's statement and some discussion the Council confirmed that licences to hunt deer on National Trust land would not be re-issued. No discussion of the scientific validity of the report was permitted since legal proceedings were still in train.

Subsequently the proceedings were withdrawn by agreement, each side paying its own costs. The Council did not however seek to ban hunting on the Dunkery Estate, covered by the covenant in the Deed of Gift.

But matters did not end there. None of the Exmoor landowners followed the example of the National Trust, and its neighbours strongly objected to its action since they were afraid that, if there was widespread shooting on Trust land, the deer would move on to their land. The Trust's own farm tenants, who by their leases were prevented from shooting deer, formed an association and claimed compensation for deer damage to their crops and fences, as a result of which the Trust has now assumed the obligation of maintaining fences and every year pays a substantial sum for deer damage to its farm tenants. The Wessex Regional Committee had not been informed before publication of the recommendations in the Bateson Report, so no alternative method of deer management was in place. The Trust appointed a stalker, Charles Harding, in an attempt to cull the deer and prevent poaching on the Estate. All this has increased the cost of deer management to the Trust, which is additional to the cost of the Bateson Report itself – about £350,000.

But the main criticism of the Council's decision was that it ignored the clearly expressed wishes of Sir Richard Acland, the donor of the Estate, and reneged on the assurances which had been given by the Trust over the years that there would be no change in the status quo at Holnicote so far as hunting was concerned. This outraged many Trust members who were not Hunt supporters. One non-hunting landowner said to me, "Having no children I have been thinking of leaving my property to the National Trust. Not now, after the way they have behaved at Holnicote."

In 1998 Charles Collins, a distinguished surgeon, and his barrister wife, Jo, who live at Crowcombe near Taunton, set up an organisation which they called "FO National Trust", or FONT. Meaning "Friends of the National Trust". Membership was open to members of the National Trust and its objects were to sponsor Council members who were more country orientated so that Trust policy would be more friendly to country life, and specifically to reverse the decision on staghunting at Holnicote. The first AGM after the formation of FONT was at Cardiff. A coach drove round the town before the meeting bearing a large notice, "Do you trust the Trust?" This was FONT's message: that the present management of the Trust was untrustworthy. Hunting members came from all over the country, especially from Exmoor, and many speakers were critical of the decision of the Council to ban hunting. In fact it dominated the meeting. Since then FONT has gradually increased its influence on Trust policy; there are now six members of Council put forward by FONT, including Charles Collins himself, who was recommended by the present Chairman. Charles Nunneley and Martin Drury have now resigned and been replaced by Sir William Proby and Dame Fiona Reynolds.

But at Holnicote relations between the Trust and the Hunt remain uneasy. There is still a feeling that the Trust was motivated by its desire to get rid of the staghunting issue, which was becoming an embarrassment to it and which, largely through its own fault, has caused it much trouble and expense, while disregarding the real issue, namely the long-term welfare of the herd of wild red deer on Exmoor. Relations between the Trust and its tenants and neighbours have been adversely affected. The only beneficiaries of this unnecessary and expensive exercise were Nunneley and Bateson, whose knighthoods both appeared in the same Honours List. Two typical Blair appointments.

CHAPTER VIII

The Hunting Act and After

LTHOUGH THERE had been many Private Members' Bills designed to ban hunting, it was not until 1997 that New Labour, led by Tony Blair, made a manifesto commitment to give government time to a bill seeking to ban "hunting with dogs". By this time the British Field Sports Society had been replaced by the Countryside Alliance. This sought to broaden the defence of field sports by linking them to other rural issues, such as the closure of village schools and post offices, and the comparative lack of rural public transport and social services, and emphasising the conservation benefits of field sports as well as their economic and social advantages. Instead of the previous defensive attitude of the BFSS, the Countryside Alliance sought to gain the initiative with high-level publicity. A mass rally was held in Hyde Park and a march through London which attracted nearly 500,000 people. Whereas for years opinion polls had shown that 70% of the population thought that hunting should be banned, an opinion poll now found that 59% thought that it should not. The D&SS was at the heart of this campaign, and local rallies were held at centres such as Exeter and on West Country race courses.

The response of the Government was to appoint yet another Committee of Enquiry under Lord Burns, a former senior civil servant, "To inquire into the practical aspects of different types of hunting with dogs and its impact on the rural economy, agriculture and pest control, the social and cultural life of the countryside, the management and conservation of wild-life, and animal welfare in the particular areas of England and Wales; the consequences for these issues of any ban on hunting with dogs; and how any ban might be implemented. And to report." The Committee was given about six months in which to complete their inquiry, and their report was published in June 2000.

As the report stated, the Committee was not asked to recommend whether hunting should be banned, nor to consider moral or ethical issues. Most of the report was concerned with foxhunting, but under the heading "animal welfare" they discussed the evidence of both Professors Bateson and Harris and concluded, "Most scientists agree that deer are likely to suffer in the final stages of hunting. The available evidence does not enable us to resolve the disagreement about the point at which, during the hunt, the welfare of the deer becomes seriously compromised. There is also a lack of firm information about what happens to deer which escape, although the available research suggests that they are likely to recover." The Committee also considered evidence of the comparison between hunting and stalking from the welfare point of view and concluded, "stalking if carried out to a high standard and with the availability of a dog or dogs to help find any wounded deer that escape is in principle the better method of culling deer from the animal welfare perspective. In particular, it obviates the need to chase the deer in the way which occurs in hunting. A great deal however depends on the skill and care taken by the stalker. It is unfortunate that there is no reliable information on wounding rates, even in Scotland where stalking is carried out extensively. In the event of a ban on hunting, there is a risk that a greater number of deer than at present would be shot by less skilful shooters, in which case wounding rates would increase. Consideration should be given to requiring all stalkers to prove their competence by demonstrating that they had undertaken appropriate training." The report also concluded, "It is generally accepted that red deer numbers in Devon and Somerset need to be controlled. Hunting with dogs presently accounts for about 15% of the annual cull needed to maintain the population at its present level. However, because of the widespread support which it enjoys, and consequent tolerance by farmers of deer, hunting at present makes a significant contribution to management of the deer population in this area. In the event of a ban some overall reduction in total deer numbers might occur unless an effective deer management strategy was implemented, which was capable of promoting the present collective interest in the management of deer and harnessing such interest into sound conservation management."

The report also remarked that, "Legislation implementing a ban might well pose some enforcement difficulties for the police." The reality of this was demonstrated to me when our local police inspector from Minehead visited me to discuss the problems of enforcement in the event of a ban. He said that enforcement of a hunting ban would have a low priority for the Avon and Somerset force, which was already having difficulties in the rural areas because of reduced resources. He said their priorities were established by agreement with the local authorities, and that hunting would inevitably fall below crimes of violence, burglary, car crime and drug crime. He also said that there would be practical difficulties of evidence in arresting and charging persons suspected of acting in breach of a hunting ban.

The government then introduced a bill, banning staghunting but permitting foxhunting subject to licence and stringent regulation, which was one of the suggestions of Burns. This was defeated by an amendment supported by Labour back-benchers proposing an absolute ban on all hunting. Astonishingly the Government supported this amendment in preference to its own bill. There followed a game of tennis between Lords and Commons, the latter passing the amended bill by a large majority, and the former rejecting it by an equally large majority, including many Labour peers. One of those, Anne Mallalieu QC, had become President of the Countryside Alliance. She was a charismatic speaker and a dedicated staghunter, who had bought a house on Exmoor. Both in Parliament and at numerous rallies and meetings she attacked the government and ridiculed its policy on hunting. How she managed to retain the Labour whip in the House of Lords I could never understand.

Eventually the Government took the rare step of invoking the Parliament Act to force through the bill, which became law in 2004, effective in 2005. Although there had been some talk in Parliament about cruelty, it had soon become clear that the real motivation for the bill was social. It was not so much what happened in the hunting field that the Labour back-benchers objected to, but the people who hunted. Hunting was described as a sport for "toffs", notwithstanding that a visit to a meet of the D&SS would have shown that to have been a ridiculous description. Some said that the Hunting Bill was the revenge of the Labour movement for the defeat of the miners strike, and the destruction of the coal industry by the Conservative Government of Margaret Thatcher. Gerald Kaufmann, a senior Labour back-bencher, appeared at one Countryside Alliance rally and mingled with the pro-hunting crowd, making provocative remarks. He was accompanied by a burly policeman. When he called Diana Scott "scum" the policeman said to George Witheridge, her Joint Master, who was standing beside her, "For God's sake don't hit him!" George is a highly respected farm tenant at Castle Hill and a local magistrate.

So our worst fears were realised. The unthinkable had happened. Hunting had been banned. There was talk of the D&SS having to be wound up, and many of the hounds were sent on loan to France, where 38 mounted packs were still hunting red deer. Section 1 of the Hunting Act provides that a person commits an offence if he hunts a wild animal with a dog, unless his hunting is exempt. One of the exemptions is "stalking and flushing out", for which certain conditions have to be satisfied, the first being that the stalking or flushing out is undertaken "for the purpose of (a) preventing or reducing serious damage which the wild animal would otherwise cause" to a variety of objects including crops and growing timber. The second condition is that the stalking or flushing out takes place on land which either belongs to the person doing the flushing out or which he has been given permission to use. The third condition is that the stalking or flushing out does not involve the use of more than two dogs. A final condition is that reasonable steps are taken for the purpose of ensuring that, as soon as possible after being found or flushed out, the wild mammal is shot dead by a competent person, and in particular each dog used is kept under sufficiently close control to ensure that it does not prevent or obstruct this objective. Finally the Act provides that it is a defence to show that the person charged reasonably believed that the hunting was exempt.

Most packs of foxhounds decided that it was preferable not to rely on the exemptions but to convert to trail hunting, similar to drag hunting. But the D&SS took the view that their purpose was the management of the herd of wild red deer, and that they would seek to rely on the exemption of flushing out with two hounds. Many experienced staghunters thought that this would be impossible and that two hounds would never be able to move the deer and keep them moving. At first the mounted field dropped dramatically, and the visitors practically stopped coming. But thanks to the skill and devotion of the Hunt staff, who all remained in place, the first season was surprisingly successful. The D&SS killed 59 hinds before Christmas 2005, as compared with an average of 7 to 16 in previous years. The technique of using two hounds is of course quite different from using the whole pack. There are more guns, and the deer are shot sooner. No deer escapes wounded, although very rarely a second shot is required. Long pursuits no longer occur. There is more lifting of the hounds. That is not to say that hounds do not follow the scent left by a retreating deer. They do, and it may appear to an uninformed or biased observer that they are being chased to the point of suffering, but they are not harassed and they are shot as soon as it is safe to do so.

The result of this has been that the popularity of deer hunting has, if anything, increased since the ban, and large mounted fields are once again following the D&SS.

The League Against Cruel Sports have of course reacted to this by "monitoring" every meet with video cameras, attempting to obtain evidence of a breach of the Hunting Act. So far only one case has been brought by the Crown Prosecution Service against the Hunt, at the instigation of the RSPCA led by its Director-General Jackie

Ballard, whom it was generally thought lost her parliamentary seat at Taunton because of her very public anti-hunting views. This case has now been adjourned because of the uncertain state of the law. A private prosecution by the League against the Quantock Staghounds was successful, and the decision was upheld on appeal by the Crown Court. But a similar case again the Exmoor Foxhounds, although successful before the magistrate, was reversed on appeal to the Crown Court, the judge holding that the terms of the Act were so uncertain that it would not be safe to uphold the conviction. So at the present time (2008) the law is uncertain and it would be pure speculation to try to forecast what the final legal position will be.

Meanwhile, although foxhounds seem to be able to live with trail hunting, from the point of view of deer management exempt hunting with two hounds is unsatisfactory. It is true that far more hinds are being culled than was previously the case, but I cannot help wondering whether the support will be forthcoming to enable the D&SS to continue. And the important role of the Hunt in dealing with injured deer is unsatisfactory. It needs four or five hounds to ensure that deer are roused, and they lie so close that many wounded deer must be missed. So the only hope for the wild red deer will be a government with a parliamentary majority sufficient to repeal the Hunting Act, possibly replacing it with an act requiring Hunts to be licensed, as originally proposed by the Labour Government, but with more realistic criteria for licensees.

The cruelty issue will inevitably be raised, and must be dealt with head on. As the Burns Committee said in their report, cruelty is comparative, once it is accepted that deer need to be culled. Deep sea fishing involves tons of fish being bumped along the bed of the sea in a trawl, which must cause great suffering. Abbatoirs must be terrifying places for animals, especially the perfectly legal kosher abbatoirs for Jews and Moslems. The whole sport of fly fishing involves torturing the fish with a hook lodged in its mouth. And I could not defend the commercial rearing of thousands of young pheasants to be driven over the guns, and many of them wounded. I would rather defend staghunting than any of these. The deer is either

Riding into the future with the Staghounds. Spot the "toffs".

killed or goes free. (And it is the natural form of culling for predators to chase deer and kill them.)

Above all, hunting should be a matter of individual conscience. It is not for Government to decide matters of that kind. To ban hunting absolutely would tear the heart out of Exmoor. It must be prevented. As the Hunt motto has it "Prosperity to Staghunting", and long may it last for the benefit of the deer.

D&SS Chairmen and Vice Chairmen

1897-1899	Stucley Lucas
1897-1899	Viscount Ebrington, Vice Chairman
1899-1932	Viscount Ebrington, KCB (became 4th Earl Fortescue in 1905)
1932-1953	5th Earl Fortescue, KG, PC, CB, OBE, MC
1941-1953	G. St C. Pilcher, KC, MC (knighted 1942), Vice Chairman
1953-1985	B.M. Waley-Cohen (knighted 1956, baronet 1961)
1953-1969	Miss B.K. Abbot, Vice Chairman
1969-1974	Colonel L.M. Murphy, OBE, Vice Chairman
1974-1985	E.R. Lloyd, Vice Chairman
1985-1995	E.R. Lloyd
1985-1995	T.A.H. Yandle, Vice Chairman
1995-	T.A.H. Yandle
1995-	T.W. Rook, Vice Chairman

D&SS Masters

1936-1939	Mr S.L. Hancock
1939-1940	Mr S.L. Hancock & Miss B.K. Abbot
1940-1945	Mr & Mrs S.L. Hancock & Miss B.K. Abbot
1945-1948	Miss B.K. Abbot & Mrs S.L. Hancock
1948-1949	Miss B.K. Abbot, Mrs S.L. Hancock & Mr M.C. Houlder
1949-1951	Miss B.K. Abbot & Mr M.C. Houlder
1951-1953	Mrs C.E. Lloyd & Mr H.P. Hewett, for the Committee
1953-1955	Col L.M. Murphy, OBE & Mrs D.A. Cox, for the Committee
1955-1957	Capt & Mrs D.A. Cox
1957-1958	Mrs D.A. Cox
1958-1963	Col L.M. Murphy, OBE
1963-1964	Major N.H. Hambro & Mr R.H. Nancekivell, for the Committee
1964-1969	Major N.H. Hambro & Mr R.H. Nancekivell
1969-1972	Mr R.H. Nancekivell & Mr S.J. Westcott
1972-1974	Mr R.H. Nancekivell
1974-1976	Mrs Norah Harding (formerly Mrs D.A. Cox)
1976-1981	Mrs Norah Harding & Mr M.E. Robinson
1981-1987	Mrs Norah Harding, Mr M.E. Robinson & Mr Maurice Scott
1987-1991	Mr & Mrs Maurice Scott & Mr P.E. Hawkins
1991-1995	Mr & Mrs Maurice Scott & Miss Mary Lycett Green
1995-1997	Mr & Mrs Maurice Scott & Mr P.E. Hawkins (died in office 1997)
1997-2000	Mr & Mrs Maurice Scott
2000-2007	Mr & Mrs Maurice Scott & Mr W.G. Witheridge
2007-	Mr & Mrs Maurice Scott & Mr W.G. Witheridge
	Mr Rupert Andrews & Miss Francesca Bell

D&SS Huntsmen

1855-1870	Jack Babbage
1870-1889	Arthur Heal
1889-1901	Anthony Huxtable
1901-1916	Sidney Tucker
1916-1937	Ernest Bawden
1937-1951	Alfred Lenthall
1951-1961	Sidney Bazeley
1961-1963	Bill Lock
1963-1971	Walter Perry
1971-1991	Dennis Boyles
1991-	Donald Summersgill

D&SS Harbourers

1855-1868	James Blackmore
1868-1894	Andrew Miles
1894-1922	Fred Goss
1922-1938	Ned Lang
1938-1946	Hector Heywood
1946-1954	Ralph Slocombe
1954-1955	Charlie Harding
1955-1962	Bill Harding
1962-1971	Edgar Webber
1971-1972	Peter Cox
1972-1976	Sidney Bazeley
1976-1981	Maurice Scott & Donald Pile
1981-1983	Donald Pile & Lionel Scott
1983-1990	Lionel Scott & Frank Dallyn
1990-1991	Lionel Scott, Frank Dallyn & Charles Parker
1991-1997	Frank Dallyn, Charles Parker & Dennis Boyles
1997-	Martin Lock, Andrew Gill, Kevin Atkins, R. Govier & A. Webber

D&SS Secretaries

1855-July 1882	S.H. Warren
July 1882-July 1887	James Turner
July 1887-April 1894	Arthur C.E. Locke
April 1894-May 1914	Philip Evered (Everard 1905)
May 1914-August 1914	G. Lawson
August 1914-May 1915	P. Everard
May 1915-May 1919	H.G. Thornton
May 1919-October 1919	H.G. Thornton & Capt G. Lawson
October 1919-August 1921	H.G. Thornton
March 1923-August 1928	Capt E.C. Lloyd
August 1928-May 1929	Capt E.C. Lloyd & Capt E.F. Wilton
May 1929-April 1937	Capt E.F. Wilton
April 1937-July 1938	Capt P.H. Greig
July 1938-April 1940	A.D. Stoddart & A.J. Collings
September 1939-April 1940	Miss B.K. Abbot & H.P. Hewett
May 1940-April 1946	H.P. Hewett & B.N. Waley-Cohen
May 1940-April 1953	B.N. Waley-Cohen, Hon Treasurer
May 1946-April 1947	Lt Col J.W. Harper
May 1947-April 1952	E.R. Lloyd
May 1952-April 1958	Col L.M. Murphy, OBE
May 1958-April 1960	R.L.V. Wilkes, CMG
May 1960-April 1964	Maj N.H. Hambro & R.D.S. Carpendale
May 1964-April 1967	R.D.S. Carpendale
May 1967-April 1970	R.D.S. Carpendale & J. Gardham
May 1970-April 1974	R.D.S. Carpendale & Mrs N. Harding
May 1974-April 1975	R.D.S. Carpendale & Walner Robins
May 1975-1976	Walner Robins & Mrs Anne Chanter
May 1976-1977	Mrs Anne Chanter & Peter Cox
August 1977-1984	J.S. Barnard & Peter Cox
August 1984-1989	Peter Cox & P.J. Lloyd
1989-1990	P.J. Lloyd & Dr J.D.W. Peck
1990-1991	Dr J.D.W. Peck & Mrs Anne Hosegood
1991-1995	Mrs Anne Hosegood & Mr J. Dibble
1995-2004	Mrs Anne Hosegood & Mrs Janet Ackner
2004-2007	Mrs Janet Ackner & Mrs Pat Bawden
2007-	Mrs Janet Ackner & Mr Nick Webber

The Staghunting Song of Exmoor

The Forest above and the Combe below,
On a bright September morn!
He's the soul of a clod who thanks not God
That ever his body was born!
So hurry along, the stag's afoot,
The Master's up and away!
Halloo! Halloo! we'll follow it through
From Bratton to Porlock Bay!

So hurry along, the stag's afoot,
The Master's up and away!
Halloo! Halloo! we'll follow it through
From Bratton to Porlock Bay!

Hark to the tufters' challenge true,
'Tis a note that the red-deer knows!
His courage awakes; his covert he breaks,
And up for the moor he goes!
He's all his rights and seven on top,
His eye's the eye o' a king,
And he'll beggar the pride of some that ride
Before he leaves the ling!

Chorus

Here comes Donald bringing the pack,
Steady! he's laying them on!
By the sound of their chime you may tell that its time
To harden your heart and be gone.
Nightacott, Naracott, Hunnacott's passed,
Right for the North they race;
He's leading them straight for Blackmoor Gate,
And he's setting a pounding pace!

Chorus

We're running him now on a breast-high scent,
But he leaves us standing still;
When we swing round by Wistland Pound
He's far up Challacombe Hill.
The pack are a string of struggling ants,
The quarry's a dancing midge,
They're trying their reins on the edge of the Chains
While he's on Cheriton Ridge.

Chorus

He's gone by Kittuck and Lucott Moor,
He's gone by Woodcock's Ley;
By the little white town he's turned him down
And he's running by open sea.
So hurry along, we'll both be in,
The crowd are a parish away!
We're a field of two, and we've followed it through
From Bratton to Porlock Bay!

So hurry along, we'll both be in,
The crowd are a parish away!
We're a field or two, and we've followed it through
From Bratton to Porlock Bay!